Growing,
Older

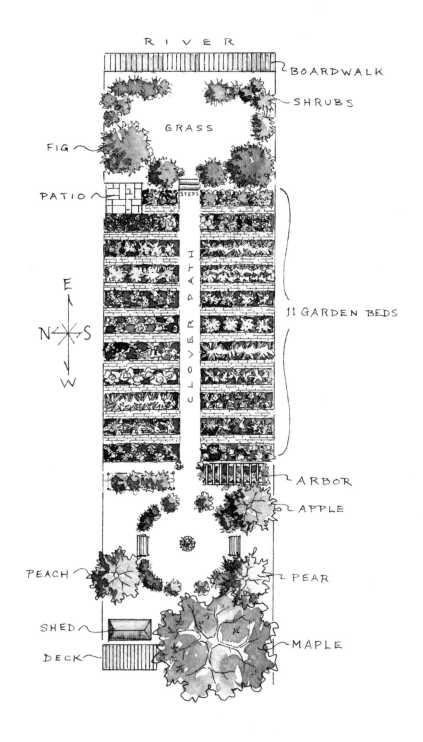

RIVER

BOARDWALK

SHRUBS

GRASS

FIG

PATIO

STEPS

CLOVER PATH

11 GARDEN BEDS

E
N · S
W

ARBOR

APPLE

PEACH

PEAR

SHED

DECK

MAPLE

Growing, Older

A Chronicle of
Death, Life, and Vegetables

JOAN DYE GUSSOW

Chelsea Green Publishing
White River Junction, Vermont

Project Manager: Patricia Stone
Developmental Editor: Joni Praded
Copy Editor: Laura Jorstad
Proofreader: Helen Walden
Designer: Peter Holm, Sterling Hill
        Productions
Frontispiece Map Illustration: Elayne Sears

Printed in the United States of America
First printing September, 2010
10 9 8 7 6 5 4 3 2 1   10 11 12 13 14

Chelsea Green Publishing is committed to preserving
ancient forests and natural resources. We elected to print
this title on 30-percent postconsumer recycled paper,
processed chlorine-free. As a result, for this printing, we
have saved:

14 Trees (40' tall and 6-8" diameter)
4 Million BTUs of Total Energy
1,313 Pounds of Greenhouse Gases
6,325 Gallons of Wastewater
384 Pounds of Solid Waste

Chelsea Green Publishing made this paper choice because
we and our printer, Thomson-Shore, Inc., are members
of the Green Press Initiative, a nonprofit program dedi-
cated to supporting authors, publishers, and suppliers
in their efforts to reduce their use of fiber obtained
from endangered forests. For more information, visit:
www.greenpressinitiative.org.

Environmental impact estimates were made using the Environmental Defense Paper Calculator.
For more information visit: www.papercalculator.org.

Our Commitment to Green Publishing

Chelsea Green sees publishing as a tool for cultural change and ecological stewardship. We strive to
align our book manufacturing practices with our editorial mission and to reduce the impact of our
business enterprise in the environment. We print our books and catalogs on chlorine-free recycled
paper, using vegetable-based inks whenever possible. This book may cost slightly more because
we use recycled paper, and we hope you'll agree that it's worth it. Chelsea Green is a member
of the Green Press Initiative (www.greenpressinitiative.org), a nonprofit coalition of publishers,
manufacturers, and authors working to protect the world's endangered forests and conserve natural resources. *Growing, Older* was printed on Natures Book Natural, a 30-percent postconsumer
recycled paper supplied by Thomson-Shore.

Library of Congress Cataloging-in-Publication Data
Gussow, Joan Dye.
  Growing, older : a chronicle of death, life, and vegetables / Joan Dye
Gussow.
    p. cm.
  Includes bibliographical references.
  ISBN 978-1-60358-292-6
  1. Gussow, Joan Dye. 2. Agriculturists--New York
(State)--Piermont--Biography. 3. Women agriculturists--New York
(State)--Piermont--Biography. 4. Vegetable gardening--New York
(State)--Piermont. 5. Organic gardening--New York (State)--Piermont. 6.
Old age--Psychological aspects. I. Title.
  S417.G87A3 2010
  613.2092--dc22
  [B]
                     2010032212
Chelsea Green Publishing Company
Post Office Box 428
White River Junction, VT 05001
(802) 295-6300
www.chelseagreen.com

To Mother Nature,
Who sometimes makes it hard,
But always makes it worthwhile

CONTENTS

PROLOGUE

I never planned to write anything like a "sequel" to *This Organic Life*. After five years of work on that book, I'd had my say about the problems in the food system that first led me to grow my own. There was, of course, no shortage of garden topics yet to reflect on. Some of the plants with the longest history in my garden were missing—zucchini, for example, the poster child for the overproductive gardener. And I'd devoted no time to asparagus or beets or kale or broccoli or rhubarb or brussels sprouts—or cranberries, for that matter—some of the other crops whose culture I have struggled to master in my small plot.

Yet despite its vegetable emphasis, *This Organic Life* was never meant to be just a gardening book. It began, after all, with the finding, gutting, and tearing down of a house. The story of that house's rebuilding, and the laying out of the garden that still sustains me, took up just four chapters. The remainder related the lessons I had learned from growing food on the west bank of the Hudson in the teeth of floods, woodchucks, drought—even my husband's death from cancer.

But woven persistently through all these meant-to-be-engaging stories were passages reflecting the concerns that underlay the entire enterprise, my conviction that we USerians urgently needed to become more local and seasonal—more conscious—eaters. We had to start noticing where our food came from, I urged, so we could reduce the negative impact of our food choices on the planet, on the people who grew our food, and on our own health. What was it that our species needed to learn about food if we were to survive to the end of the twenty-first century? That was the real subject of the book—my rationale for writing about the garden.

Yet lurking around the edges of those horticultural morality tales was another, much less obvious story that for a time ran parallel to the one I was writing down, a story I was trying *not* to tell. The fact behind the other story was not disguised—namely that early in the course of my work on *This Organic Life*, Alan, my devoted husband of forty years, had died suddenly of cancer. In several chapters I revealed his too-sudden death almost in passing, in a manner that, happily, most readers seemed to find touching. Some people, in fact, reported to me that they read the book as a love story: two devoted people gardening together, one of them dying, and the survivor soldiering on. Which turned out to be a partial truth.

The larger truth—my shocked discovery that I didn't miss Alan after he died—led to months of guilt and years of trying to write myself into an understanding that friends insisted I needed to share. "Other people feel that way too, Joan, but no one says it." You, however, will be spared reading about most of those struggles, only a small portion of which have ended up in this book.

This book is made up mostly of other things: what I thought about after I learned I didn't miss Alan, and some of what I have been thinking and doing in the years since. *Growing, Older* is, really, a book about growing—in this case the growing of a life-sustaining garden on the west bank of the ever-flooding Hudson River and the growing maturation of the aging gardener—me—who nurtures it. It features my often amused reflections as I strive to grow older happily in a rapidly denaturing, novelty-obsessed world.

Largely retired from an academic life, and drawing strength from the chronic demands of a garden that feeds me, I reflect in successive chapters on how—lacking a partner's assistance—I deal with everything from broken appliances, bodily decay, thoughtless travel, and experiential obsolescence to repeated floods, muskrats, and river trash. Most of all, perhaps, I steadily deal with the disparity between the ideas I live by and incoming messages about how an "elderly widowed woman" ought to think and behave. Scattered throughout are urgent suggestions about what growing older on a changing planet will call on all of us to do: learn self-reliance and self-restraint, yield graciously if not always happily to necessity, and—since there is no other choice—come to terms with the insistencies of the increasingly unnatural world our choices have left us with.

This book is about my life path, about companionship, about being alone without being lonely. It's about how to be hopeful despite the increasingly alarming future of the planet, about how I've made it through my first eighty years and what I plan to do with the next twenty should I live so long. The story includes vegetable production, of course, since that is a significant part of my life, and there are reflections on the inescapable reality of growing older, a reality that inevitably affects the garden enterprise that keeps on giving both substance and meaning to my later years.

JOAN DYE GUSSOW
AUGUST, 2010

I

The End of
My Marriage

To be no longer content to pick up what is floating on the surface of life, and to want only the
pearls at the bottom of the sea, this is grace,
welling up from deep inside.

—EKNATH EASWARAN

CHAPTER ONE

The Death of My Husband

It was late afternoon of December 19, 1996, when my husband Alan came home from a visit to the doctor who had read his CAT scan—a "fishing expedition," in the doctor's words—and told me he had a fatal cancer. I was sitting at the computer then, working on God knows what. He came home after dark, slamming the outside door, and my first thought was that it was a celebratory slam, that he was arriving home with good news. I said "Hi," and he crashed into my office crying and shouting, "It's terrible, it's terrible," leaning against the door frame. "I have cancer of the pancreas and it's spread to the liver." We both knew it was a death sentence, one that would be quickly executed with little time for appeal. I leaped up and hugged him and cried. He kept saying, "It's unreal, it's un*real* . . ." And of course for a while it was.

We spent the whole evening numbly making marmalade from home-grown grapefruit I had chopped up the night before, when our life had a long horizon, and then boiled twelve hours later on the morning of Alan's devastating visit to the doctor. If the fruit wasn't sugared and cooked down now, it would have to be thrown out. Boiling marmalade was the perfect task for that endless evening; it gave us something concrete and satisfying to focus on.

We made twelve half-pints and two quarts and all of it jelled—which says something about patience when your world has stopped. It says much more, probably, about not wanting to face the night. We went off to bed when the marmalade was done, and I took a sleeping pill to fall asleep. Alan, a reliably gifted sleeper, didn't—but his place in bed was empty very early. Our grief at that moment was numbing.

We had been planning to leave for Cuba right after Christmas, for an agriculture-focused tour around Havana with a group called Global Exchange. And when the gastroenterologist, on Alan's second visit, told us that there were no miracles available and that the usual time from diagnosis to death was five to six months, he assured us that delaying treatment—if any—for a week or so would make no difference. So we decided to go ahead and live our lives. I wrote in my journal:

> **DECEMBER 21** Everything's changed. But nothing has changed. I'm still me—I've promised to continue to nag him—and we had a dark laugh about the fact that I wouldn't have to nurse him through the Alzheimer's that took both his parents. Alan kept saying it was so unreal. It is. It is. He's so healthy. The doctor had just said so—like a man ten years younger. His pulse is like an athlete's. No high blood pressure, low cholesterol, good wind. He's strong as hell. And God knows we eat better than most people. And our own crops—no pesticides—for at least 25 years! It's random.

After thirty-six years in a giant house twelve miles north of where we were now, we had moved—less than two years earlier—to the edge of the Hudson River in Piermont, and as we digested the doctor's latest words, Alan kept saying how happy he was in our new home and how much he wanted to see our newly created riverfront garden beautiful and finished. "I can't do it alone," I said tearfully; and tearfully he replied, "I don't want to leave you alone." And I keep trying not to think of being here alone, doing it all alone, having no one to share my life with. "Alan is dying," I wrote in my journal. "How can I write that? How does one even process it?" And then I lectured myself: I couldn't let myself cry anytime I felt like it. I couldn't let myself think of things that made me cry or I would make it impossible for Alan to hold up.

We agreed that we couldn't tell our sons about Alan's illness until we returned from Cuba, when we'd be around to help them deal with it. That meant we had to keep the awful news from anyone who might let it slip. Alan did call a doctor who was a close friend, swearing him to secrecy. When he got off the phone, he reported that Marvin had given him from a month to a year. "I either lost five months or gained six," he said.

Accustomed as I was to blurting out my life to friends, I found the necessity to keep the terrible news a secret an added strain.

> **DECEMBER 23** It's so strange that one of the things that's hardest at the moment, and most stressful, is answering the phone and when people ask how we are to say "Oh, fine!" We can't tell anyone. But when Kathy called and asked "how are you?" and I said "OK, how are you?" she said "OK," and laughed. "Both guarded aren't we?" And I said, "Are you going to the Midwest for Christmas?" She was. I said "Can you keep a secret, completely, since you will be out of town?" She said yes. So I told her.
>
> She was incredibly appropriate, not even losing her sense of humor. It was a great relief, to cry and let her cry and get that tight lump out of my chest that comes both from thinking about the future and having to lie about the present. It's so difficult to think of how to tell people so as to cushion their grief.

A couple of days later I wrote in my journal that I had "a great tightness in my chest all the time trying not to think ahead." And as I sat at my desk, one morning when Alan had gone for "a guided biopsy of the liver," thinking about how we were supposed to grow old together, I burst into tears. He was supposed to get cranky and difficult and absentminded and I was supposed to get tart and snappy about it, but we were supposed to be out in the yard together and treasuring our new life. Now it was ending.

We joked often about my having to learn where to buy things. But it's true; he shopped delightedly. He took such care of me— even when I didn't want it. And we did share values, care about the same things, work toward the same goals. And here we are in Piermont, I thought, but it's over before it's actually had time to settle. I was grieving for the life we would not have. I was grieving for all the things I anticipated from our old age. I was grieving for the whole future we wouldn't enjoy. "And now," I wrote in my journal, "having wiped my eyes one more time, I'll go back to my 'disciplined Joan' game and do all the other things I have to do so that we can go to Cuba and I can give my speech in California and so on, and so on, and so on." And except for the diversion of Cuba, things went downhill from there.

But nothing that happened in those painful following days prepared me for a truly shocking event that occurred just six months after the diagnosis. Two or three weeks after Alan died, I found myself headed to the local store on a beautiful May morning—skipping down the street. "My God, Joan," I gasped—probably out loud—"what *are* you doing?"

Trying to figure out what I was doing was what first provoked this book. Forty years earlier, when I was a happy but displaced California girl ready to set down roots in 1950s New York, I had been eager to marry this handsome smiling artist. And now, after the memorial service had ended and the crowds of friends left me alone, I found to my stunned surprise that I was still optimistic about my future—unexpectedly sanguine about living without him.

It wasn't that our marriage had been unhappy—by all normal measures it was successful. But only I seemed to know the Alan I had actually lived with all those years, the preoccupied, often unoccupied and depressed man who contrasted so starkly with the charming artist who projected himself onto the world. Much more than I realized, it had been a strain for me to support the whole edifice of our family life—financially as well

6

as emotionally—while Alan intermittently painted, consistently charmed outsiders, and kept everyone at bay.

I had never seriously considered leaving him, but now that he had exited through forces that no doctors, treatments, or loving care could forestall, I found myself feeling little of the grief that friends (and I) anticipated once my "denial" wore off. My intrinsically optimistic nature seemed to have survived intact through the years of our marriage, and was still there when I was left alone—ready to pilot me through my later years. As I came ultimately to understand, my conviction that I'd had a long and happy marriage was not a delusion; for most of those forty years, I lived a truly happy life. The surprise was that so little of my happiness had depended on Alan.

CHAPTER TWO

Six Months Later

Years after Alan's death, I stumbled across a letter I had written to an old friend of mine, living in Japan, just six months after Alan died. When I found it, I had just spent five years trying to put down on paper how I really felt just after I became that standard object of pity, a widow. I was still struggling to understand how I could lose my husband of forty years to cancer and catch myself two weeks later skipping down the street. And I was still trying to figure out why I felt the way I felt. To my surprise, the letter said it all.

OCTOBER 29, 1997

. . . How am I? As I have just personally discovered, Americans are very conflicted about death and really can't face it. Even now, six months after Alan died and almost a year since I knew he would, people who don't know me well assume I am in a fragile state. I am not, so I want to tell you a little about my state of mind. Your openness to the possibility of complex emotions—which came through so well in your letter—encourages me to be totally honest with you.

It has been such a strange time for me, John, not as you might imagine, because I am having so much difficulty learning to live alone, but because I am finding living alone such a deep pleasure. The first few weeks after Alan died, I had so much trouble with my feelings. At first, I thought I was just relieved. Since he had died at home, without ever going to the hospital, it was obviously easier when the stress of having a dying person in the house was over. I kept thinking that one day I would fall apart.

Finally I realized that I simply didn't miss him, that I was, in fact, quite happy. And having that feeling seemed quite unacceptable. How could I not miss someone to whom I had been married—presumably happily— for forty years? You know me; I am painfully direct. I couldn't fool myself, but how was I to cope with the fact that all around me were people assuming that I must be absolutely prostrate, people who would approach me with tears in their eyes, desolated by the death of this energy-filled, always publicly positive man?

I actually went to see the therapist to whom Alan had gone for a kind of death consultation (though I'm not certain Alan ever accepted the fact that he was dying) and said, "I've come because I'm not missing Alan." And he said, "And you're feeling guilty?" And I said, "Well, not exactly guilty, but I'm having to cope with the Saint Alan phenomenon, and I can't figure out how to deal with other people." So he told me that I had to have one story for my close friends, and another story for everyone else. It's really hard for me not to be honest, but I made up a phrase to use for people I felt I shouldn't be frank with. "I'm doing very well thank you, considering the circumstances. Thanks for asking." When I tried that on my friends, they said, "Oh, come on, Joan. How are you really."

Sometime when I see you, we may talk about some of what I learned in successive moments of revelation— moments when I would do by myself something that Alan and I would have done together and would realize with a start that most things were easier without him. The persona he projected, always optimistic, always flattering, always engaged and energetic—was not who Alan

9

really was. Much of what he really was appeared in those beautiful and touching works of art he created; but that part of his life was very private. (His may be the only artist's children who were never invited into Daddy's studio to do drawings.)

I played a very special role in his life drama, one which often had little to do with who I actually was, and over which I had almost no control. I was cast as his father (he himself said this), the person he needed to please, and he played what had been his mother's role in his family. He was always "available," always apparently attentive, while at the same time, he used his social skills to maintain his privacy. He also hated his dependence on me . . .

I guess one just adapts to a lot of things in a long marriage, and if anyone had asked me six months before he got sick if I had a happy marriage, I would have said, "Of course."

One recent day, all my thinking led me to the sudden recognition that the reason I didn't miss him was because I was very used to living alone, and that I had been doing it for a very long time. I am a person who needs intimate emotional relationships, and I don't think I really ever had one with Alan. Luckily, I made lots and lots of friends with whom I could share almost anything, and I suspect that saved my marriage. And luckily for Alan, he developed that shining persona with which he could earn rewards in the world even as he kept the world at bay.

So that is where I now am, John. I continue to adjust to my life alone, learning what I cannot do by myself—go for long car trips for one, put lightbulbs in our ten-foot ceiling (even on a ladder) or transplant heavy trees— and what I can do if I think it through first. I capture guests to help me with the impossible things. I usually don't enjoy this time of year despite the fall leaves, so we'll have to see whether I'll become more depressed as the fall closes in and the days become shorter.

Warmly,
Joan

The first November after Alan's death and the winter following—the indoor months—were a strange time. The anticipated "end of denial" never arrived, but the human world outside my house was treating me gingerly, tenderly, sensitive to my very recent loss. Nature, however, in her own inexorable way, continued to give me whatever she chose to hand out—floods and all—indifferent to my new status. And I was not feeling Alan's absence as the acute and chronic emptiness I had anticipated. I kept experiencing it as a strange liberation—from things I hadn't known I was imprisoned by.

SEPTEMBER 6, 1997 . . . the only reason I need to analyze my reactions is to understand why I don't miss him. Yet? I don't know if it's "yet." Will he return in a different form? Will I come to remember the person everyone else remembers and find that I miss that person? What I have missed, I find, is the notion that he is in there doing that marvelous art. When I catch sight of one of his things— like that brook pastel upstairs—I realize that it came out of some deep spirit. And that spirit is gone. But on a day to day level, I don't miss that spirit because I never experienced it in his behavior toward me. Toward me, he was almost always anxious, distracted, dependent.

OCTOBER 3 But there's no doubt about it. I do feel liberated, out of my chrysalis, able to be myself. A huge part of it is body rhythms. I always knew that when he was away I moved around the house differently.

NOVEMBER 30 It's Sunday night and I had just started to read the Sunday *Times* book review when I noticed that there was a book about Americans trying to make better sense of death. And I found myself, for one of many times today, thinking about Alan and who he was and why during this holiday season that everyone thinks will be awful for me, I don't feel awful at all, but rather happy. I told someone earlier today that I was thinking of going into therapy to find out why I feel so good. They laughed.

Risking the mal-interpretation that others' dream recountings invite, I need to comment here on an astonishingly revealing dream I had only a few weeks after Alan died. The morning of the dream I awoke at four thirty and turned on the radio, hoping whatever was on would put me back to sleep. But as I started to listen, dream fragments came trickling back and I realized that rather than distract myself, I should try to recapture it; this was the first Alan-centered dream I could remember having had since he got sick.

In the dream I was lying on my back in bed, grubbing a bit of lint out of my navel, when suddenly a string of stuff began to ooze out. I pulled and pulled and it kept coming out, a long, thin tape-like thing that must have been five feet long when it was finished. I pulled very carefully so as not to break it.

When it was done, I realized in the dream that, early as it was, Alan was already out of bed, and I got up with the tape hanging over my arm and went in to tell him about it. I found him shaving and asked him why he was up so early. But I couldn't get his attention; he seemed to be preparing for something or getting ready to go someplace and couldn't listen to me—focused inward the way he always was when he was preparing for a "performance" out in the world.

I wanted to tell him what had happened, show him what I had found because I thought it was funny. And I realized that if I did finally get Alan's attention and tell him my dream, he would act as if he had heard what I was saying, and say something like "That's funny," but he wouldn't really have heard me.

And as I lay in bed recovering the dream, I started giggling; abruptly I had understood what it was about. I was dreaming about Alan's umbilical connection to me, about his inability to leave me alone when I needed aloneness, to the point where he could not let me get up or go to bed alone—even when he himself craved isolation. In Congers, where we had lived for thirty-six years before our move to Piermont shortly before Alan's death, I would very often be in my second-floor office working after dinner, and he would be sitting up on the third floor watching TV. When I decided I wanted to call it a night, I would switch off my light (a silent Mercury switch as it happened) and pad quietly down the carpeted hall past our bedroom to the bathroom to wash up and brush my teeth. By the time I got back to the bedroom, he would already have come downstairs and be tucked in bed—and sometimes nearly asleep. It was actually spooky—and irritating.

Years earlier I had experimented with the other end of the night, making my only open attempt to have some time alone. The boys were both under four and I was desperate to have a few minutes to myself when no male, young or old, was competing for Mommy. One evening I realized that if I got up an hour before Alan and the children woke, I could go down, make coffee, and sit and read without feeling that I was stealing time from anyone.

So I did it. I don't remember if I set the alarm, but I got up quietly, slipped on a bathrobe, went down to the kitchen, made coffee, and read. It was perfect. I remember the deliciously unaccustomed peacefulness I felt at being alone with myself, even briefly, before all the boys got up. Definitely worth repeating.

But the next morning, when I got out of bed, Alan sat up, ready to rise, too. "Oh Alan," I said pleadingly, "please don't get up. I need to be alone."

"I'm not going to bother you," he said. "I'm just going up to the studio."

"I know," I told him (thinking several other things!), "but I really need to feel that there's no one awake in the house who might make a demand."

"Well, what do you want me to do?" he said in irritation. "Am I supposed to just lie here awake?"

"You never get up this early."

"Well, I'm up. I can't just lie in bed." And so on. And thus ended my dash for freedom.

So my dream was quite explicit about the thing I used to feel—and occasionally say—when Alan seemed to come to bed or get up in wordless synchrony. I would say, "I feel as if we're connected by an umbilical cord at the navel." Now, after his death, I was pulling out the cord.

And so the fall and winter came, and the New Year.

JANUARY 3 (1998) And just now, around 6:45, I looked out and realized that there was going to be a wonderful sunrise, so I put on my jacket and went out to stand on the boardwalk and watch it. It was as beautiful as any I can remember—indeed, standing there watching the little black ~~~ in the sky that were the birds flying, I remembered standing with Alan watching the sunrise in Quorn that morning in Australia.

And then I thought about Alan and wondered whether I would have been able to stand out here with him this morning in the same way . . . He couldn't be quiet when we were together. If we were in the same space, he was almost always talking, even if he was really distracted and absent (though physically present).

I am embarrassed now to remember that once in a burst of frustration I blurted out quite unkindly that I hated being with him in the garden because he couldn't just *be*. It upset him, of course, and I had to retract the statement with fulsome reassurances. But I found it quite maddening that he was always asking me what needed to be done out there, when he had no intention of doing it. Because the fact, not obvious to observers, was that as much as Alan loved the garden, and loved showing it to visitors, he was an artist and was actively resistant to planning—wary of being controlled by a list of tasks-to-be-done, or even Nature herself. So even though he was never making a mental list, as I often was when we walked the garden, he loved to comment on the things we saw that needed doing. He kept asking questions when what I wanted was just to be quiet, just responding to what Nature was saying.

Which is, I am sure, one of the reasons I found myself so content the summer immediately after he died; I could just *be* in the garden without responding to him or trying to find something to keep him busy and out of trouble. That latter sounds, I recognize, like I was treating him like a child. Was it me? I really don't know. But I think I just felt smothered by his demanding inattention.

One of our sons once said after Alan had died, "Dad's life goal was to perform Alan Gussow and he was brilliant at it." There is perhaps no single moment that so clearly illustrated his truly desperate drive to perform as the morning, five days before his death and well beyond talk, when he walked down our outside staircase to the river. Several people who had not seen Alan as he failed, and others who wanted to see him again before he died, came out from Manhattan one morning for a last visit. By that time he had been moved to a permanent hospital bed in the upstairs living room, as I could no longer help him get downstairs to our bedroom. One of the visitors that day was Hazel, a seriously religious woman who had been his family's longtime maid, and who was very devoted to Alan.

While she was fussing over Alan—by this time quite discolored from jaundice—commenting on how handsome he still was and how he still had his familiar little smile, I went outside with one of the visitors. A few minutes later, our son Adam came rushing out and said his dad had announced that he was going to "walk to the water." "He damn well isn't," I said, and dashed upstairs. Hazel was transported, explaining excitedly how he had awakened from a sound sleep and announced that he was going to walk to the water. I said he couldn't do that since he could hardly walk, and I leaned over and gently told him that he could sit on the terrace in the sun, but couldn't go downstairs.

So we set up a chair on the terrace and a friend took one arm and Alan's brother took the other and we led him out. As I moved a chair over to the railing so he could sit there, he pushed hard left toward the stairs. It is very difficult to do physical battle with a dying man, so with much support on both sides Alan made it down the stairs, where Adam put a chair under him on the deck. He sat for a few minutes and then got up and moved down the path—again with someone on each side. Halfway down we sat him down again (Alan uttered not a sound through all this), then helped him up again until he made it to the riverbank and sat down.

He stayed there only a few minutes before getting up and heading back, with the same band of attendants supporting him holding a chair behind until he reached the house. We led him around to the main entrance, helped him go inside where there was a railing to hang on to as he climbed the stairs, and got him back to bed. Hazel, meanwhile, was interpreting his every move spiritually and knew she had seen an act of God. Irreligious Alan, performer until death, had played the saint for her. I'm certain he would have walked *on* the water if he could have managed it. Five days later, without ever having spoken more than a few terse words, he died.

It was sometime early the following spring that I scattered Alan's ashes in the garden, an event I was later surprised to discover that I had not recorded in my journal. I remember that I picked the day because it was quiet and lovely out, and I was alone—and it just seemed the right time.

I had opened that crematorium can—like an unlabeled can of paint—only once before, when my older son Adam wanted to take some ashes to scatter off Monhegan Island where Alan had spent many painting summers. But that time it was in haste and in company that I scooped some of the gray and surprisingly gritty ashes into a Baggie and put the lid back on. Since then the can had sat in its shiny maroon bag under the small desk in the sewing-bill-paying-filing-laundry room, reminding me whenever I sat there to write checks that I needed to deal with it.

I really hadn't wanted to open it again, perhaps because I felt that then, if ever, I would begin to mourn—or fall into grief at not mourning. But once I pried off the lid, it was easy . . . I put some of the gritty ashes on the strawberries, and some on several of the beds, saving two handfuls for the river. And although I expected to feel Alan there, I never did. I only wondered again where—if anywhere—he was, and once again had to acknowledge that my greatest sense of loss in those days arose from the fact that I so seldom thought of him and *never* again dreamed of him.

As the months passed, and my mind continued to expand into its newly private space, I found that the ongoing effort to understand my unexpected state of satisfaction affected everything I thought and read.

MARCH 7 Just finished reading Carol Flinders's book about faith and feminism, *At the Root of This Longing,* and found myself in tears. It is a wonderful book, profound and truthful and wise and honest and all those good things—plus witty. Just about when she brings you to a point where you don't think you can follow her erudition, she backs off and says in effect, "Well now, do you really think *I* wanted to spend four days a month for the last 40 years shut up while menstruating?" and then she leads you further.

The first passage that made my eyes water was when, in talking about women exerting efforts to "recapture a tradition of female strength and dignity," she observed that we needed "to understand the basic elements of the ceremonies designed to sustain a culture that honors women." And then she lists them. "Sequestration at regular intervals in a female space . . . special songs and dances . . . the laying on of hands . . . adornment . . . athletic prowess . . . instruction in life skills . . . self-mastery . . . deferential support of menfolk . . . communion with divinity . . . opportunity to serve the community . . ."

And as I mentally checked my life against each phrase, I was overwhelmed with how extraordinarily lucky I had been—in choosing a career in nutrition (which surely sequestered me in a female space, initially much against my will—I had been a pre-med after all!); in loving to sing and dance when I was young and in spawning a blues harmonica player; in having lovely women doctoral students whom I could hug and advise; in my athletic California childhood, which left me unsurprised that adult women could sweat; in the confidence I gained from knowing how to cook, clean, sew, crochet, knit, garden, and (thanks to my son-less father) hammer, mix cement, repair lamp cords, and take pleasure in doing all these things; in learning early how to make do with little material wealth; in having a husband who was unthreatened by any confidence I gained; in working in a professional community (and now living in a geographic community), which give me opportunities to serve. In a conventional sense, I have lacked only adornment and communion with divinity, although I am always proud to wear soil on my hands and believe that when I am in the garden I am communing with Mother Earth.

I have been feeling strong, and wondering why I should feel strong when my husband has just died. Somehow Carol's book made it okay, and gave me a rushing sense of relief. I didn't actually burst into tears until page 313 and the line "To be capable is to be powerful." I do feel capable. And it does make me feel powerful. When the garden flooded (again!) two weeks ago, I cried a bit, and said "enough." Then I went out and cleaned up and a friend helped me fill sandbags. After an afternoon of lifting the 25-pound bags onto the boardwalk, I walked inside, saying to myself "Well, kid, you're almost 70 and you can still take care of yourself."

I'm sure that the busyness of my life—many of my commitments had been put on full-stop during Alan's last months—helped me move on into my own future. I was serving on the National Organic Standards Board at the time the very controversial first set of proposed regulations for organic food were issued, and was also on the boards of directors of several organizations whose activities demanded time and attention. Moreover, though I had retired, I still taught every fall—a large class called Nutritional Ecology that required serious rethinking every summer. And there was, of course, the endless coping with a garden, which seemed always to need me.

Almost a year to the day after Alan died, I wrote to a friend:

> Dear Gayle,
> You have been in my thoughts so much lately, as the various anniversaries have approached.
>
> Both boys came here for dinner on the . . . night of May 5 and we had a remarkably peaceful and reflective time, talking about what we missed now that Alan was

gone. I surprised Adam, I think, when I said that one thing I missed was Alan's cooking. He was a wonderful cook, and now I'm stuck with only me.

All things considered, it's been a good year. And surprising because it was less difficult than I assumed it would be. I was probably more prepared to take care of myself than many women would be after 40 years of marriage, and I have a wonderful group of very intimate friends who have been incredibly helpful and supportive. The village too was remarkable, food on the doorstep, flowers at the gate, loving concern expressed in a variety of ways. So all in all, I'm doing very well.

And so, meeting my commitments and drawing on friendships that I had brought with me through marriage, I moved into what I found myself describing to intimates as the final trimester of my life. The autumn of Alan's death I turned sixty-eight. Having had a mother who died at 94, and a cousin who was still going at 100, I certainly anticipated many more years of life; but a third trimester would take me to 102. I wasn't quite sure I wanted to go on that long.

CHAPTER THREE

Coping with Despair

Forty years of allowing me to deal with our mutual life problems had given Alan no practice at facing things. And when he finally acknowledged that he wanted no more of the experimental chemo that had multiplied his misery without in any way extending his life, his response startled a visiting friend of mine. Alan's major anxiety appeared to be that he might offend the doctor by refusing "treatment."

"Did Alan ever get the shit kicked out of him?" my friend asked bluntly as we waited for an apologetic Alan to come out of the doctor's office.

"I'm afraid not," I said. "He always managed to charm himself out of unpleasantness."

But after watching Alan die with what appeared to be an utter denial of either curiosity or open fear, only an irresistible need to perform and a too-often-expressed concern that he not offend anyone, I suppose it was inevitable that I would speculate on how I might face my own end. Since I've seldom managed to charm my way out of anything, I'm hoping I'll handle dying the way I have in the past handled other threatening events: with a certain amount of ironic discounting, some courage, and at least a trace of humor.

Meanwhile there's still the future to deal with. And I have to admit I'm feeling a great deal more hopeful about it since everything tanked at the end of 2008. I bring this up now because I have come to believe that my failure to experience despair over losing Alan is not inconsequentially related to the story I am about to tell. I'd been waiting for an economic collapse for decades because I had found it so difficult to try to adapt to living through a gilded age whose excesses I knew were devouring our planetary home.

So it's been a decided relief not to encounter headlines like the one that ran over a story several years ago describing a marina designed to accommodate yachts up to six hundred feet long: "Resorts Respond to Yacht Parking Problem." When I read that—at what turned out to be near the end of the gilded age—I wasted time calculating that ten houses the ample size of mine could fit into one of those yachts if it ever parked off my boardwalk in the Hudson River; which it couldn't, of course, because the river is too shallow here.

Around the time I read that article, I had just finished organizing the readings for a session on energy that was part of a course I began to teach forty some years ago at Columbia University Teachers College, and continue to teach in retirement. I had first put a session on energy and food into this course in the 1970s, when rising petroleum prices caused by turmoil in the Middle East had led some scholars to calculate that we were using ten calories of fossil fuel to get one calorie of food to our tables.

But some time after the price of petroleum plummeted and incoming President Reagan, declaring it "morning in America," had removed the solar panels from the White House roof, the nation returned to treating energy as a free good. My students in that era of reviving optimism were sufficiently puzzled about the fuss I was making over energy that I dropped the session, folding a few of the energy articles into a larger discussion called "The True Cost of Food."

But the summer after the six-hundred-foot-yacht article appeared, concern over energy returned—with a vengeance. This time what attracted the most attention was not an absolute shortage of fuel—there was such a furious silence about peak oil that almost nothing warned the ordinary consumer of any long-term problem with the supply—but the *price* of gasoline and heating oil. And the fallout—fall-up really—of the products of fossil fuel combustion was getting some notice, thanks partly to Al Gore.

By then, denial that the habitability of the globe was threatened by the rising levels of CO_2 and other "greenhouse" gases in the atmosphere was limited to a few flat-earthers. And an understanding began to penetrate that the approaching crisis would ask much more of us than the righteous-feeling mini conservation of the 1970s when we were, for example, warned against standing before an open refrigerator asking ourselves what we wanted to eat. This time we would be called upon to change the whole way we interacted with the planet.

My class readings were organized in relation to a series of questions to which the answers were frightening. How's the planet doing? Very badly; the poles are melting and the sea level could rise as much as twenty feet. So what's the problem? Around the world poor people who live on coasts or near deserts are already losing land, homes, and livelihoods; tropical diseases are moving north; we could be next. What were we doing about it? In the United States mostly denying the urgency; in some other places making a modest start. Are we running out of oil? We have passed or are passing peak oil; what's left will be harder—and require more energy—to get. Will we run out in time, before we disrupt the climate irrevocably? Once the economy begins to recover, energy will get more and more expensive very rapidly; but meanwhile it's cheap. And who knows if price alone can force us to change in time. What to do? Stop encouraging air travel; stop driving around on weekends looking for a place to be happy; grow and eat local food; don't just recycle, use less; stop reading the ads, buying stuff, and throwing it away. Change *fast*.

Taken as a whole, the readings communicated a sense of urgency that was especially alarming given the chronic indifference and passivity toward these problems that had paralyzed our government for decades.

When my co-teacher finished looking over the readings that

come two-thirds of the way through a course that—because it considers humanity's impact on the earth in relation to the future of food—is already sober, she looked at me and said, "These are really depressing." And they are. The planet is doing very badly, heating up at such a rate that people living at the margins around the world are watching their livelihoods burn up or disappear underwater; and food chains are coming apart in unanticipated ways.

Moreover, what we 4-plus percent of the world's population who were sending up a quarter of the CO_2 were doing about the problem was shamefully little, especially given the scale of the crisis. The last Bush Congress could not bring itself to demand raised mileage standards for automobiles, yet the reality of what was coming if we kept on with business as usual was, quite simply, unimaginable. As a consequence, most people seemed unwilling to try to imagine it. The environment was *not* at the top of the list of worries for most people, although climate change had risen to the top among environmental issues, but in the face of financial meltdown, even that level of concern collapsed.

And yet—I feel awkward confessing this before I have time to explain it—I was not depressed by the story the readings told, even though the frightening 2007 report of the International Panel on Climate Change (IPCC) had arrived on my computer screen labeled "Here it is, the future of the world in 23 pages." I recognized my own sense of relief in the face of this daunting future prediction during a call from a dear friend who has been with me on much of my journey through reality hell. After we shared the news that the "Synthesis Report of the IPCC Fourth Assessment Report" gave us ten years before we might have irrevocably tipped the planet toward runaway heating, she said, "I'm sort of relieved." And I startled, realizing that I was too.

Now, before I begin trying to explain that anomalous response, I need to take a giant hopeful breath and note that almost all the alarms I have raised to date in this chapter just might benefit from the meltdown of the global economy and the near simultaneous election of a brilliant new "change"-oriented president. I doubt very much that scarce capital is presently being expended on enlarging marinas, and although the early signs of just what Obama's "change" means in relation to energy are less than I hoped for, it is entirely possible that within the next several years, serious caps on the production of greenhouse gases will be put in place, that the burning of coal will be entirely phased out, and that the impending meltdown of the poles may be slowed. And financial collapse may slow the rate at which we consume—thereby slightly ameliorating our impact. Nevertheless, we are irrevocably headed toward living on an unfamiliar planet, in circumstances very different from those any of us is used to.

So how is it I was relieved to hear the sobering verdict of the climate change experts? I said earlier that the happiness of my marriage appears to have arisen from the happiness of my life, a life in which I seem able to go on year after year teaching about the ever-more-likely end of the world as we know it while remaining a fundamentally happy and optimistic person. The reason is not, as the greenhouse deniers would have it, that I simply hate Late Capitalism and hope that this particular crisis will at last shut it down—although, as the post-Bush financial meltdown has so vividly shown, it may come close. I do hate the frenzied consumerism chronically encouraged by the conviction that only "growth" will save us. I do hate the fallout from what we have been taught to call progress. But my relief derives from something much more complex. And to explain it requires a loop backward, this time more than a quarter of a century, to an event that occurred nearly a decade after I had begun teaching Nutritional Ecology.

I had begun instructing in 1970, as a doctoral student, and had against all odds become department chair two days after my oral even as I continued to teach huge classes, one of them Nutritional Ecology. This course connected the increasingly absurd US food marketplace—in which product introductions had swelled by the end of the last century to seventeen thousand a year—to such global environmental issues as hunger, global limits to growth, the fallouts from pesticides, the loss of farmland, and the centrality of energy in the food chain. The first few sessions of the fall semester—during which I brought mostly bad news to students—always left me not only tired, but depressed.

By the fall of 1979, fifty-one years old and due for a sabbatical, I was exhausted. The new semester was about to begin, and I had asked one of the previous year's students to be my class aide. She said she'd think about it. A week or so later she came into my office to tell me that she had considered turning my offer down, since she'd found my course the previous fall so hard to get through. At first unsure if she "wanted to go through all that again," she decided to accept partly because of an article she then handed me. "You seem very tired," she said. "Maybe this will help." The article by eco-philosopher Joanna Macy was titled "Coping with Despair." I thanked her, jammed her contribution into the pile of paper already stuffed in my overfilled backpack, took it home with all the other things I had to read, and didn't think of it again until the next morning.

In those days my solution to the problem of having to commute to Manhattan by car was three twelve-hour days at the office, interspersed with Tuesdays and Thursdays at home, barring an urgent meeting at work. On Mondays, Wednesdays, and Fridays I got up at five thirty, beat the traffic in, and followed it out. On at-home days, since my children were by then away at college, I got reading and writing done without much interruption. So the following day, sitting at my desk at home, I got to Macy's article and began racing through it to get to the next thing in my backpack. I never made it.

Macy was reflecting on the difficulty of remaining hope-filled if one tried to confront the environmental and nuclear perils of the time. Then she told a personal story. In preparation for a workshop on the nuclear threat, she had spent an evening reading materials about the horrors of a post-holocaust world, and went to bed sobered and depressed. She fell asleep and dreamed that she was holding her children's hands and walking in a barren landscape that, as she looked ahead, became a field of ashes. In the dream she understood that she needed to let go of her children's hands and allow them to move forward into desolation. Then she woke up. Getting out of bed, frightened and shaken, she walked into the bedroom where her seventeen-year-old daughter was sleeping, laid her head next to her daughter's on the pillow, and said in a trembling voice, "I had a bad dream." I burst into tears.

And I couldn't stop crying. Entirely overcome, I sat sobbing hopelessly at my desk. Finally I got up, wandered into the bedroom where Alan was sitting on our bed reading, and tried to tell him what had happened. But I wasn't sure what had happened. I only knew I couldn't stop crying. I had a despairing few hours. At one point we both went downstairs and outdoors, and I sat tearful on the porch steps while he—not knowing what else to do—decided to take our garden cart and go down the street to a place where two immense white pines did their annual fall molt right next to the street. Every autumn, when our own giant white pine displaced last year's needles with new growth, surrounding itself with a fragrant brown carpet, we went down the street to rake more pine needles off the pavement for mulching our rhododendrons.

After Alan went off with the broom rake and cart, I remember sitting on the porch steps staring red-eyed into the sky next to our pine tree and imagining that if the bomb were to detonate overhead right now, the yearly needle drop might never happen again. A nuclear war . . . a nuclear winter, and this repeating marvel of Nature could be stopped forever. And I began again to weep. I knew for the first time what it meant to say your heart was broken. Destruction of civilization, even of our own species, seemed nothing compared with the fact that we might wipe out the remembered round of seasons. It might really be too late to save the planet—at least any planet we would recognize.

It took more than a few days for me to understand what had happened: After ten years as a teacher, I had suddenly internalized the implications of what I had been saying in the classroom. In my first years of teaching, as I kept developing my Nutritional Ecology course, I was learning new things every day, having what were to me thrilling new insights. I was connecting what all of us put in our stomachs to topics never before considered part of nutrition. I was excitedly creating my own cognitive frame around food, taking the surfaces apart to see what was underneath, and reconfiguring the facts to make a new picture of the staggering long-term costs of our almost ludicrously abundant food system. The intellectual challenge of creating a new field was sufficiently engaging that I had found no time to stop and ask what it all meant. It was one thing to create the picture. It was another thing to believe in my own creation.

And now, abruptly believing it, I could scarcely bear my own truth. It took me several weeks to settle down. I remember how grateful I was to have a guest speaker for the following week's class, since I knew I could not yet teach without talking about what had happened to me, and I had no desire to dump my own grief on students. So I kept it to myself, although I tried in a variety of ways to help the students deal with their own emerging pain as they worked through the readings I had brought together. Almost three decades later I still sometimes tell that story to my classes as they begin feeling their own despair. Sometimes I even manage to do it without tears.

What tempered my grief in the short run was something Macy said toward the end of her article—which I finally got around to finishing. She asked a spiritual counselor whom she knew well what one could do when one no longer had hope. He replied, "You have possibilities." We know so little about what really produces change in our world, especially when Nature is involved. We know that human inventiveness can produce solutions as well as problems. To assume the worst *will* happen is almost as wicked as plunging ahead trying not to notice what *is* happening under our noses. That understanding has sustained me ever since.

Everything is possible. Living with possibilities allows me, most of the time, to face deeply disturbing truths about the state of the planet. And I know that the friend who called me, almost elated by the bad news from the climate change experts, has worked out some equivalent method of dealing with what she knows. Now that the headlines occasionally carry the truths I have lived with for close to half my life, the relief is that I can talk about them and not be thought mad.

And there is something more. Reflecting on my early confrontation with despair has helped me to understand my failure to seriously grieve after Alan's death. Losing him was not the worst thing that could happen in my world. That I had already confronted.

CHAPTER FOUR

Taking the Red Pill

The brilliant novelist, essayist, and poet Barbara Kingsolver once said when asked how she coped with what she knew:

> I focus on two different levels: an empirically based scientific level that tells me we are in an absolute mess, and a spiritual level in which I remain hopeful, giving to my kids, and doing something about the mess. At the end of the day, the science view sometimes seems to be winning, but in the morning, I wake up with hope.
>
> Hopelessness is, I think, a selfish abdication of responsibility for the future, an institutionalized form of child abuse. The cynicism of this culture is purposefully eroding our empathy and compassion and our children's psyches as well. . . . I take in as much as I can manage, and look for a way to feel valuable. I think that's a need as basic as sleep and nutrition—the hunger to feel useful.

Many years ago, walking from one building to another at a professional meeting, I ran into a student whom I had not seen in a number of years. We chatted on the sidewalk until she suddenly pulled away: "Joan," she said, "you know my husband and I have been living very frugally since I took your class. We try to save energy and materials and we recycle anything we can. But it's been a number of years and my husband wants to know when *is* the world going to end?"

I laughed, sensing that she wasn't utterly serious, and said "I really don't know." But the implication was there for both of us: During the 1970s when she took the class, it was premature—

even if foresighted—to conjecture about where our inability to stop assaulting the planet was taking us. Now that we find ourselves on the brink of irrevocably damaging the control systems that keep earth habitable, nothing one can say seems really premature. So it's much easier for me than for most people to accept the IPCC's warning that we have maybe ten years to transform ourselves.

Ever since I began teaching the course my former student was referring to, I have been the regular and grateful recipient of articles or clippings that add to my understanding of one or another of the issues the course touches on. One memorable addition was a collection of newspaper articles on the concealed use of toxic wastes as "inerts"—that is, "inactive" carriers of the nutrient substances in fertilizers—as a way of disposing of wastes profitably. This brilliant series from the *Seattle Times*—later a book[1]—arrived on my desk by way of a student who had come across it when she visited friends in the Northwest.

Like those articles, most of my printed gifts come from present or former students, or colleagues. And I acknowledge with some regret that what has come to me by this route over the years is very often grim news about humanity's assaults on our global environment to add to my already overlarge collection.

But it is my serendipitous approach to wisdom accumulation that I want to note now, since it accounts for a major "aha" moment about Alan, provoked by one of those messages from somewhere that appeared on my desk unbidden a couple of years ago. It was a reprinted article called "Escaping the Matrix" by Richard K. Moore, which set me thinking furiously, not least because it turned out to have first appeared, three years earlier but unnoticed by me, in a magazine I claimed to read regularly. So *that's* what lurks in all those unread piles!

Moore described himself in a footnote as a Silicon Valley expatriate, and his article made the case that we citizens of the modern age are living in a "fabricated collective illusion," about who and what really runs the world. Although I agreed with much of what he said, I introduce him only because in his opening paragraphs he described the "defining dramatic moment" in the film *The Matrix,* the moment when Morpheus invites Neo to choose between a red and a blue pill. The blue pill will allow him to continue living in any way he wants. The red pill will allow him to see the truth. Taking the red pill, Neo sees that in the real world, humanity is asleep, "cocooned in grotesque embryonic pods," sources of energy for the society's rulers.

My first reaction on reading this was that I needed to see a movie that seemed likely to speak to my sense of painful separation from a nation in deep denial. (Alas, it failed utterly to speak to me—wrong generation, I suspect.) Meanwhile, I carried the red and blue pills around in my head for several months until, in a conversation, they knocked loose a profound understanding about my personal life.

It's crucial to make the point here that, in some very basic way, Alan never understood how my teaching had transformed me. His reaction when he saw my first set of readings in the early 1970s was to say quite nicely that I didn't know enough to teach it. My grateful response was that I knew that, but it needed to be taught. And if I didn't teach it, I said, nobody would. And Alan's response when I had my epiphany about the state of the world was, as I noted, to go and rake pine needles.

He was proudly aware, of course, that I went on to teach my difficult insights for all the years of our marriage. He even thought up the title of the book of readings and essays I derived from the course—*The Feeding Web.* But as I knew from living with him for forty years, there was a sense in which he never came to believe—as I did after my Joanna Macy epiphany—the sobering picture my life work painted.

And so we come back to Alan's swift death from pancreatic cancer. Having failed to feel the grief I had expected, I was, several years later, carrying the newly discovered red and blue

pills around in my head. I shared their story with a wise therapist, someone from whom I was hoping to learn something more
about (1) why I hadn't missed my husband when he died, and (2)
how to be an old person. I'm not sure why I was telling her about
the red pill/blue pill scenario, but she looked up at me and said
quietly, "I see. So Alan took the blue pill, and you took the red
pill." And I said out loud *"Wham!"* as the pieces fell into place.

Of course. That explained so much. I was always scrambling
around trying to get to the bottom of things—figuring out what
seemed to be "really" going on, and anguishing about the ills
of the planet. Alan, on the other hand, had a profound need to
believe (or seem to believe) that the world—human and otherwise—was just as it appeared to be, with everyone liking him,
everyone having honorable motives, and so on. He left all suspi-
cion, all bouts with reality, to me. Since he managed his public
world so smilingly, and so deftly controlled the situations in which
he interacted, there were only a few occasions when life brutally
asserted that his self-created picture was not the real world. On
those occasions, he was always deeply shaken and depressed.

Except when he wasn't; except for the occasions when his
capacity for denial astounded even me. Most memorable was
the time when I cautiously informed him of an event I thought
would seriously roil his calm, only to have him appear quite
unaffected. In 1989 Alan and I each spent a month of adventure, apart. I had been asked to teach in Tokyo, in a master's
program in English as a Second Language headed by a faculty
friend from my university. And while I lived my amazing adventure, immersed in Japanese students and culture, Alan had the
opportunity to travel to El Salvador as part of a delegation from
CISPES (Committee in Solidarity with the People of El Salvador)
bringing to the war-ravaged refugees of that nation funds that
had been raised through an art benefit that Alan had helped
plan. The delegation consisted of Alan and five young women. I
felt confident there was safety in numbers.

Apparently the trip was fairly hazardous and the group frequently had to work out ways to shake their minders so they could meet with dissident locals. On one occasion they drove through Salvadoran army lines, pretending to be American tourists, and ended up in a little village, San José Las Flores, in the mountains of Chalatenango where as they slept overnight in a church they heard bombs falling nearby. Next day, they set up crude wooden ladders and—directed by the villagers— did a mural on the outside wall of a church, a mural carrying symbols of both wartime devastation and the residents' hope for a better future. Having finished painting, they went off to dinner and came back in the dark to find the villagers gathered with lanterns by the church, singing to the mural. Alan's account of the adventure was deeply moving.

A month or so later, both of us back home, I saw a small item in the paper about the destruction of a village in the mountains of El Salvador and was horrified to see that it was San José Las Flores. I grabbed the paper and raced upstairs to Alan's office to tell him. I wondered whether the mural had been destroyed, and what had happened to the villagers. But Alan didn't seem to wonder anything. He seemed utterly unfazed. He said something like "Oh, really. That's too bad." And that was it. In retrospect, I'm certain that he cared. He was just unable to let himself confront the impact of terrible events.

So the red pill/blue pill metaphor helped me understand, at last, what had on the deepest level isolated me from Alan. To a truly remarkable extent, we were interested in the same global problems, and our areas of expertise overlapped rewardingly as many people noted: He was trying to keep the natural world intact with art; I was trying to save it with food. We once took a sociological test to assess our values and came out eerily similar; it's just that we looked at the world from wholly different emotional perspectives. I took our planet's environmental distress really seriously; he couldn't. He could verbalize his anxieties about what was happening to the world, but he couldn't really let them affect his emotions. He could admire my passions, but he could not share or even really understand them. My belated recognition of that solved a hundred puzzles that had littered our marriage.

One of these was his behavior toward consumption. A child of the Depression—as he was—I had been trained to careful use from infancy, and was reinforced in that stance by marrying an artist who never earned enough to make wastefulness a realistic possibility. I was genuinely proud of my frugality and the way in which it allowed us for many years to survive—even thrive—on a poverty-level income. Although it was frustrating then to have him view anything he earned as "extra" money to be spent in ways I thought indulgent, I put that down to habits carried over from his chronically shopping mother.

I arrived at a different interpretation very late in our marriage. Something in our kitchen had broken—I can't now remember what it was—not the toaster that my parents had received for their wedding, which was still working perfectly, having been repaired by my father in the 1940s. This was something much smaller, and Alan's response was that we should throw it away and get another one. "We can probably fix it," I said, to which he responded, "But new ones are less than ten bucks." And all of a sudden I realized that after all my years of worrying about our nation's wasteful use of the world's stuff, all my talk about "reducing throughput" and conserving—things that even my students accepted and tried to live by—Alan still didn't get it.

"It isn't the money," I almost shouted, wondering how to get through to him. Now that I was a department chair, we could certainly afford much more than ten dollars, but what the planet couldn't afford was all this buying, briefly using, and throwing out, this trained consumerism. "Can't you see that after all these years it isn't the money?" I suspect whatever had broken was made of metal, since I ended up ranting on about the fact that someone, somewhere had a miserable life, ripping up the earth to mine the chrome, and so on and on.

Yet despite my frustration, I am certain that the next time something broke, he probably bought a new one even before I could object. Not to do so would have required him to take an entirely different look at the world, and for what I now understand were fundamental reasons, he couldn't. He had chosen to take the blue pill.

And I, of course, have taken the red pill, and Alan's death has left me free to become, as I age, even less tolerant of this planet-heedless consumerist society than I was when, as a young adult, I could be made to want things despite my best intentions. And it has left me free to be happy. Once when I remarked to a friend that I felt guilty about being so happy despite knowing how much of a mess the world was in, he replied, "Joan, if you're not happy, why would anyone want to listen to you?"

I mentioned to my students the other day that they would not find many people who wanted to hear what they were learning in our class. "Your boyfriend will not want to hear about it, and your father will tell you your teacher is misled. If you know an economist, she or he will tell you I am crazy. These are not things people want to know." Then I added, "That's why I'm so lucky. I get paid for you to come and listen to me tell the truth that no one else wants to hear. I have an outlet!"

And so do they, I keep reminding them. They have youth and energy, access to knowledge and enough common sense if they use it to help rescue the often senseless world they are inheriting. They do not have to fight their own way though the thicket of nutrients that fenced off their predecessors in the nutrition profession from learning how to love and understand whole food systems from farm to table. All around us now the food world is shifting, and the next generations are at exactly the right place to influence that change.

And I—determined as I am to remain in touch with the

seriousness of the crises the human race is rushing toward—I teach to stay sane, and I stay happy by growing food in a riverside setting so beautiful I never take for granted that it's mine to cultivate. The regular flooding of my garden, when the Hudson overflows its banks in response to storms, keeps me in touch with the steady rise of the seas. I battle back by producing food there anyway, hoping that my determination to keep on keeping on—despite what I know—might at least serve as some piece of a model for how we can gracefully yield to Nature in the hard times to come. Which is what I wrote to a former student and fellow worrier about the world after my last giant flood:

> There are moments when I think this whole enterprise is doomed to defeat, but then the sun comes out, the garden re-emerges from the river, and I resume. This time will be a mess. Some of the raised beds have floated up—at one end, and the water at one point was over my 18" wall! It's all very sobering—and does remind me, as I intend this self-provisioning adventure to do, that we are not in charge and had better save every resource we have for the times ahead.

$\overline{\text{II}}$

What Next?

Tell me to what
    you pay attention
and I will tell you
    who you are.
        —JOSÈ ORTEGA Y GASSET

CHAPTER FIVE

Moving the World Around

Of the many things that confront you when you lose your life companion of so many years, one of the most unexpected is realizing you've lost a source of power. Without being aware of it, I had come to assume that if I couldn't lift, or move, or turn on something, I could always round up Alan and ask him to help—or leave it and ask him to do it later. It was often *much* later that it got done, but when, with his death, *later* permanently became *never,* I was forced to recognize that there are tasks you simply cannot accomplish alone.

I know that there are many women, at least in my pre-health-club generation, who always found someone else to do what are usually designated male jobs. I was not one of them, at least partly because my father trained me to be his son, and partly because for most of my adult life, we couldn't afford much hiring out. I'm pretty strong for an old lady. In the course of trying to raise my vegetable beds above the water table (high here, on the shores of the Hudson) and stop the flooding from my neighbor's property to the north, I've lifted a lot of too-heavy pavers and heaved a lot of twenty-five-pound sandbags up onto my boardwalk from the beach, leading friendly observers to comment that I'm an unlikely candidate for osteoporosis.

But there are things I can't manage. After trying a few times to pull my large dirt-loaded garden cart up and over the four-by-four riser that separates the driveway from my yard, I had to learn to ask for a push from someone working in the community garden next door, or—lacking such assistance—unload enough bucketfuls of dirt to make the heave-up possible without a second set of muscles. Moving the giant rhododendrons behind my house to allow for some reconstruction required the strong backs of some accomplished plant-moving friends.

And from time to time, people much larger than I am—most of them men—show up unasked, volunteering to help with the heavy chores. On such occasions, I'm always amazed that young masculine muscle can so speedily accomplish what it would have taken me half a morning to accomplish alone—if I could do it at all. Yet in the end, even with testosterone-bulked muscle and energy on tap, there are tasks well beyond the physical capacity of one or even two strong humans.

I first learned to think in such manpower terms on Monhegan, a Maine island, ten miles out from the mainland, where my husband's family, and now my sons and sister-in-law, have owned a house for more than half a century. There are no motorized vehicles on the island except for a few trucks that carry luggage, groceries, fuel tanks, and end-of-season lobster traps from the dock to wherever they belong. And since the trees in the island's woods are all protected, the occupying humans haven't been able to do much to alter their environment except move rocks and soil.

So over time a tradition arose: The rocks you could move when you wanted to make a house—or a garden—were called "one-man rocks," "two-man rocks," and "three-man rocks." And during the years I was regularly on Monhegan in the late 1950s, three-man rocks established the limit of what could be rearranged.

A few years later an actor bought some property near ours with the intention of building a house on what was, in its natural state, sloping land. To what extent his fame determined the outcome I can't say—certainly his cash helped—but he arranged to bring a bulldozer ten miles across the ocean on a barge to help prepare his homesite. And inevitably, once the bulldozer was there, people thought of all sorts of things they wanted to do. A neighbor of ours built a swimming pool right down by the shore out of giant neighboring boulders; other people leveled the land around their houses and built extensions. The power to rearrange the planet's surface had come to the island—but only so long as the bulldozer stayed. Once it floated away, Monhegan's much-remarked-on slow pace of change was restored.

That the planet's reordering is for the most part no longer constrained by such limits in most places accounts, I think, for our sense of being overwhelmed by the transformations around us. The inhuman powers that easily accessible petroleum has enabled our species to control for a little over 150 years have allowed us to move around many more parts of the world—from molecules to mountains—than we have learned to be responsible for. And our human tendencies to multiply and travel have spread the products of our material restlessness over much of the surface of the earth.

My understanding of what this implies about our species' relationship to our surroundings was primed by something I read long ago, in a surprisingly unremembered book by the psychologist Philip Slater,[2] about the dolphin's lack of hands. I seem to recall that it was in a discussion of human arrogance where he pointed out that a remarkably large slab of the human cortex was occupied by neurons that accepted sensory information from the hands and sent motor signals back out to them.

Physiological psychology text books, he remarked, featured a picture of a human figure, with the parts so scaled as to reflect their exact representation on the surface of the brain. It is a childlike figure with a large head, a tiny body, and giant hands hanging from skinny little arms. Why the disproportion? Because, Slater pointed out, it is the abundance of messages to and from our hands that allow us to feel and, more uniquely, manipulate the world we inhabit. As a consequence, a rapidly expanding part of our world is manu-factured, literally "hand-made."

Dolphins, who also have large brains, don't have hands. They can't manufacture anything. Except for a bit of fin-carrying and nudging about, they can only live in and interact with the world as it is. Which led Slater to ask: What do dolphins do with that giant brain when they can't manufacture anything? Perhaps, he speculated, they communicate, surely a provocative idea since they can't "talk"—or write—but at this point it is a diversion. What I want to emphasize here is the unique dominance of our handiness.

Given our manipulative capacity, we and our primate ancestors long ago figured out how to use what we now call tools to extend our hands' power to change things. Apes use sticks to get at termites, and early humans learned, among other things, to use logs as pries to move objects much larger than three-man rocks.

Over the centuries humans also discovered external energy sources to extend their powers. Those most familiar to our immediate ancestors were animals, wind, fire, and water. Of these, wind and water were quite place- and time-determined, and fire—if not carefully controlled—could be dangerously unmanageable. So for much of our history, harnessed animal power accounted for much of the human-instigated work done by other than human muscles. As recently as 1850 in the United States, for example, "domesticated animals—horses, oxen and mules—were responsible for about 65 percent of the physical work supporting the economy."[3]

And then there were fuels, especially the portable ones. As it happens, fuel energy in the United States has a short unique history. To start with we had wood to burn beyond believing. Economist Kenneth Watt made this point strikingly clear by explaining that on a pristine continent covered with trees, we were, by 1850, using fuel per capita in pounds of coal equivalents at levels that Switzerland and Japan (two of the most technologically sophisticated countries on earth) did not reach until 1969.[4]

In 1974, at the time of the first modern "energy crisis"—when the Organization of Petroleum Exporting Countries (OPEC) cut off petroleum supplies—Watt looked at US history through an energy lens, and noted that this nation had been endowed with uniquely abundant fuel supplies: wood, coal, whale oil, and ultimately petroleum. Each had come into use before the prior one ran out, a piece of luck that taught us, inaccurately, that energy was cheap and relatively easy to get and replace, and that we could forever use some form of it at will to move the world around in whatever ways we wished.

As a consequence, we have used energy lavishly to support a growingly profligate lifestyle. And in pursuit of more of everything, we have become so proficient at using fossil fuels and the things we make with them to rearrange parts of the world—from damming rivers, to air-freighting perishable produce around the world, to pushing whole mountaintops into valleys to get at the coal seams underneath—that we find ourselves on the brink of irrevocably harming the control systems that keep our planet habitable.

Those in charge have been painfully slow to recognize these facts with anything like the necessary urgency. In 1978 I wrote:

> There is a familiar "chase" sequence from my childhood that still turns up regularly on TV's Saturday morning cartoon shows. In it the chasee somehow lures the chaser into running off a cliff; the pursuer's momentum carries him (never—oddly enough—her) off the edge of the cliff and—still running—out into mid-air. Suddenly he realizes where he is, looks down—and falls.[5]

Then, and now, our heedless dash off the cliff has been enabled by abundant supplies of artificially cheap fossil energy.

Those of us anxious to extend our species' stay on the planet are convinced that we have, thirty years later, dashed even farther out from the cliff edge—still running on air—and we realists (called pessimists in some circles) find reasons for optimism in recent warnings that humanity may be coming to the end of cheap oil. Anyone sufficiently diverted by the media circus not to have noticed how many natural systems seem to be coming apart will undoubtedly find it deeply alarming that what we've defined as "progress" may be braking to a juddering halt. In fact, it actually offers a kind of hope, especially in regard to the food supply.

At the time of the first modern fuel crisis, way back in the last quarter of the twentieth century, our nation—and the world—faced a fuel shortfall that briefly altered everything about our lives. We noticed it because it came on dramatically—as the result, as I said earlier, of an abrupt cutback in oil production by the then newly formed OPEC. The sudden high price—and shortages—of oil, which shocked us first at the gasoline pump, went on to shock us at the grocery store, the hardware store, the garden shop, and even the clothing store, since the price of everything was affected by the price of the energy that it took to produce and move it. One place where the effects were markedly visible was in our food.

The energy in our ancestors' food was produced by the sun, with an assist from solar-powered human and animal labor, but that fact is obscured in our current food supply by the dominance of products increasingly remote, literally, from their roots. Everything we eat that isn't a mineral (like baking soda or table salt) comes originally from processes in which solar energy and—in the case of our industrial food supply—fossil energy is transmuted into substances we can bite into or drink. Unfortunately, the story of that transformation is not part of our education, so we learn to view food calories not in terms of their origins, but solely in terms of their effects on growth, maintenance, and—too often, lately—body weight. Yet it is cheap and apparently limitless fossil energy that has shaped our present food system.

The vast lake of fossil energy on which our nation floats is largely invisible until the price of fuel for our cars and living spaces increases. So it was the rapid escalation of energy prices during the 1970s that briefly made visible the extent of fossil energy's support of the food system. Ecologist Howard Odum wrote at the time that we had ceased, during the last half century, to eat "potatoes made of solar energy" and had begun to eat "potatoes partly made of oil."[6]

That oil, embedded in petroleum-based pesticides, herbicides, and fertilizers, and in fuels for building and moving farm machinery and trucks, drove up the energy cost of growing and shipping foods—many of them obligatorily refrigerated or frozen using fossil energy—to processing plants (more energy for processing and packaging) and wholesale and retail markets (more energy for packaging, cooling, shelving, et al.). So it was that the increasing calorie cost of every food calorie was briefly made visible in food's increasing cost in the market. When the cost of petroleum went down, so did food prices and concern for the energy costs built into the food system . . . until now.

If the energy crisis of the 1970s was temporary, today's energy crisis seems about to be permanent.[7] However much oil prices may fluctuate in the short term, the long term is probably closer than we think.[8] James Howard Kunstler's book *The Long Emergency: Surviving the Converging Catastrophes of the Twenty-first Century* is his analysis of what will happen—and fairly soon—to our petroleum-dependent society as we pass the peak of all-time petroleum availability.[9] We have used up the easy-to-get half of the planet's gift, just as demand increases from developing countries like China and India; oil companies will invest more and more energy (and money) to get at remaining petroleum reserves, which will increase the cost of petroleum, reduce the net energy yield, and make harvesting it unavoidably more risky.

"Net energy" is a concept perhaps more vital to general education than the names of the original thirteen colonies, but it is even now only occasionally referred to. Compare the energy required to stick a pipe down into the sands of Texas and capture the gushing oil (remember the movie?) versus that required to build (and maintain) a huge weather-stable platform for deep-sea drilling in the North Sea or the Gulf of Mexico and to keep the rig pumping when weather damages your drilling platform—as it inevitably will given the hostility of the natural environment. At a certain point it will become "uneconomic" to get at the remaining petroleum or at many of the other presumed sources of liquid fuel—like tar sands.

As for the agricultural petroleum substitutes now being touted, there are ongoing debates about whether most plant sources can produce a useful net energy yield when they are converted into liquid energy. Any specifics on this score will be outdated as they are written, but what will remain essential is chronic skepticism about whether agriculture can be used to transition our way out of petroleum dependence cheaply—if at all. In less than two hundred years, we have used up half the entire legacy of solar energy laid down as petroleum during the life of the planet, so the notion that we can, year by year, use contemporary solar energy to grow ourselves out of the coming petroleum shortfall is inarguably absurd. Moreover, to count on flood- and drought-vulnerable farm fields to grow fresh fuel in a time of increasing weather instability may turn out to be almost as risky as counting on fossil fuel whose availability depends on Middle Eastern goodwill.

Kunstler concludes that the end of cheap oil is inevitable, and spends many pages explaining how and how much everything will change. "Food production is going to be an enormous problem in the Long Emergency," he writes.

> As industrial agriculture falls due to a scarcity of oil- and gas-based inputs, we will certainly have to grow more of our food closer to where we live, and do it on a smaller scale. The American economy of the mid-twenty-first century may actually center on agriculture, not informa-

tion, not high tech, not "services" like real estate sales or hawking cheeseburgers to tourists. Farming.[10]

If he is right, the end of cheap oil will almost inevitably move us toward the sorts of local food systems that are just now emerging around the margins of the larger marketplace.

Even if Kunstler's exact vision of the future is wrong, there can be little doubt that the end of cheap oil will mean the end of a system so energy-intensive that on the average, as I have noted, we have been estimated to put one edible calorie on the table for every ten fossil fuel calories we invest in getting it there.[11] And the end of cheap oil will necessarily constrain the casual shipping of food around the world to bring the most cheaply produced food to us rich consumers. Among other things, as Kunstler remarks, Walmart—with its far-flung supply chain—may find it difficult to remain the largest food retailer.

And then, of course, there is the fallout from burning all that fossil fuel, the effects of climate change on farming and our food supply. It is becoming increasingly evident that *not* running out of fossil fuel might be the worst thing that could happen to us, since the products of its combustion are already creating totally unprecedented changes in the climate that will, in turn, have totally unprecedented effects on agriculture—the base of our food chain.

Because it's so hard to find a tolerable way to talk about messages like Kunstler's, the growing interest in developing local food systems comes as very good news. Because while much of our society has been blindly consuming as if there were no limits on human capacity, communities across the globe have begun to talk of food sovereignty, working against the dominant trends to rebuild strong regional food systems under local control that will be able to feed future generations with food grown close to home. It was a commitment to that particular future that drove my determination years ago to learn whether I could indeed live locally, with my diet demanding a minimal input of fossil energy. I found that I could. Now some communities have already in place many of the ingredients for eating nutritiously, sustainably, and deliciously in the coming "long emergency."

It seems highly unlikely that we will return to a time when a three-man rock or a "controlled burn" marks a limit to what we humans are capable of modifying on our planetary home. Nevertheless—as a way of making more visible the vast undergrounds of petroleum and coal by which our society is fueled—it seems useful, at a minimum, to begin reflecting on how much of what we think of as human progress depends on fossil energy. There's much to be learned by becoming conscious of the sources of—and the impending limits on—our capacity to move ourselves and other things around, although thoughts about losing a husband may seem an odd way to begin the conversation.

CHAPTER SIX

Making Change: Just Do It

I had planned to have my ears pierced in my seventieth year. It seemed like an appropriate marker, though of what I am not certain—a splendid way of diverting observant eyes from the wrinkles, perhaps. Now that I've been pierced, and worn earrings on numerous occasions, I'm quite certain I look better wearing them; but I really didn't know that beforehand, only that for some reason I wanted to have it done. I think ear piercing was some sort of declaration of independence; after Alan's death I could just *do* it, without discussion, without his thinking of a downside or jumping in to find the right place to have it done.

I do wonder, though, what he would have thought. So often when I think of doing new things now that he's gone, I am reminded of how much change alarmed him. And *alarm* is really the right word, I think. Having come from a childhood of near-constant and always arbitrary and unexplained change—after all, his parents had a mover on retainer—he was an addict of routine. It was inevitably a struggle to get him to agree to change our way of doing anything even if I could prove to him that a change would make things faster, smoother, simpler, quieter, or otherwise better—household efficiency being one of my life goals.

Anyway, once I decided to have my ears pierced, I began looking for places to have it done. I went out to the local mall one day with piercing in mind, seeming to recall that there were jewelry carts lining the middle of the downstairs walkway. There were, and all of them offered piercing. Alarmingly, they all seemed to be staffed by poorly groomed, overweight, and what looked to be questionably clean teenagers to whom I was not about to trust my bloodstream. Who knew what they might communicate—blood poisoning or something worse—AIDS perhaps, or a fondness for heavy metal.

I had no clear idea of just what had to be done professionally to make ears ready for earrings, except to drive some sort of spike through—by hand? by machine? I didn't know. I believe I was told as a child that that mothers used to use a hot needle and an ice cube at home, and more than once I was tempted to give up seeking professional help and try instead to find a courageous friend.

Once during my seventieth year, I was in New York City with a special young couple with whom I often share Thanksgiving weekend, and I mentioned my interest in getting punched. We stopped in a Greenwich Village store that advertised piercing on its front window. Jennifer—gorgeous and always adventurous—noticed a sign indicating that piercing took place downstairs and went down to check it out.

As I was standing with her boyfriend, waiting for her return, I looked around at what was on the shelf behind me: dozens of videos involving the exertions of simply enormous male organs. I sensed immediately that this was not the place I wanted to be stabbed. Jennifer came back up and reported that a young woman was having her navel pierced with "a bunch of guys" standing around kibbitzing. We left. That was the most misled of my abortive attempts, but I did check out several other places that advertised they did "piercing," and none filled the bill.

One day my son came out to visit from the city and convinced me to go to the unsuccessfully opposed, big, ugly mall that I had been ineffectually boycotting in the years since it was built—a fact that seriously handicapped my moviegoing. I was fully aware, of course, that my boycotting the mall, my not-buying-with-a-purpose, caused no ripples in the smooth flow of commerce, since I so seldom buy anything anywhere, but a principle is a principle. Adam and I walked around several ugly noisy floors, avoiding the Ferris wheel and the merry-go-round, picking up a card holder for my wallet and some other little things. Then I remembered my ears. By this time I was seventy-two, so some of the thrill was gone, but my son is tenacious.

The same grungy teenagers seemed to be peopling the jewelry stalls at *this* mall, but then we came to what seemed by mall standards a rather "upscale" shop and saw inside a tall, handsome, impeccably dressed African American woman wearing a badge that said I AM A PIERCING EXPERT. It was not so much her advertised expertise as the fact that she looked clean that convinced me to make the leap. I leaped, she pierced with what looked like a paper punch, and I went out with some golden studs in my ears, a bottle of "ear care," and instructions to leave the studs in place for a month or so. My son had looked away during the entire process.

What none of my friends had told me before I got into this— and I now began to notice that many of them always wore earrings—was how easy it was to forget your newly pierced status, and fail for two weeks or so to open those tiny portals by inserting something. My struggles to get earrings into my ears after these lapses—struggles that sometimes involved drawing blood—clearly confirmed the opinions of several of my intact friends who, having grimaced at the mere thought of what I had done, flatly refused to help me find the right hole, and made clear their intent to remain unpunched ear-wise until death.

I feel obliged to mention, however, for those of advanced age considering taking this rather ordinary step, it's worth it. I *do* look better with earrings—and I know I feel better. They *do* distract from wrinkles. Best of all, my new status has given my really thoughtful friends something other than local food, homemade soap, or hand-thrown pots to give me for Christmas in the teeth of my determined nonconsumption.

CHAPTER SEVEN

Working, Out

It was the story about micro liposuction, illustrated with a picture of a woman gesturing at her bony crossed knees, that did it. I had just come in from one of my meant-to-be-brief garden look-overs and had sat down with the paper to have my granola with the last of the fresh strawberries I had picked just before dark the night before. As usual, I had gone out—aware that what I really needed to do was clean up my dismally disordered desk—just for a look. A friend who had an early appointment in New York had stayed over and was up and gone at 5 AM, so I was outside earlier than usual and figured I would back be inside by 6 or 6:30 latest. The sky was mostly cloudy but the sun was beaming broad shafts of foggy light down through a gilded slit in the clouds—a beautiful morning to stand in the garden and look out to the river. So I went out and strolled down the convalescing clover path, trying to ignore the invading grass that marred the clover's perfection and hoping that the newly sown clover would ultimately win out as it had on the riverbank, where it triumphed over a weedy mess. Adopting a "let it go" approach had become urgent since the previous summer's separation of grass blades from clover had become so obsessive that I had contemplated having to call my next writing effort *Hooked on Grass.*

But the ignoring failed—even with my elderly eyes, I could still see the tiny pink flower heads of the aptly named "smartweed" that seemed able to insinuate its way unnoticed through the clover stems, staying mostly invisible until it needed to flower. By the time I saw it, it was always multistemmed. But unlike the grass, it was easy to pull, even as an adult weed, and I found it deeply gratifying to track down and eliminate a mass of crab-like stems with one pull. So of course I had to lean down and remove weed patches, which led to sitting down on the damp clover (crouching being no longer an option for my ancient patellae) to locate every plant, and noticing in the process certain clumps of grass that were easy to yank out.

And then there were the weeds in the broccoli and brussels sprouts beds. I had taken a notebook with me to note the chores that would need doing later when I actually came out to *work* in the garden. I regularly made such lists, but all those little weed pullings were not on them. In fact, thinking back, I can't think of a thing I did that morning that was really urgent, and at one point when I realized I had lost my pen in the course of some busyness on the riverbank, and found it in a pile of weeds I had just discarded, I knew it was time to go in. I think it was seven o'clock by then. So I moved back toward the house. When I finally came in—after going back three times to pick up the coffee mug I kept leaving behind, and each time finding one more patch of weeds to pull—it was eight thirty and time for breakfast and the paper.

I glanced at the sports section, looked over House and Home, which was all about trophy kitchens, and then came to Thursday Styles. There it was on the top left—the headline "Do My Knees Look Fat to You?"[12]—a question that I must confess it had never occurred to me to ask, even in my deepest bouts of adolescent insecurity. I am at the age when I dare to hope only that all my hinges will continue to function without disabling pain until I don't need them anymore. Since, like my mother before me, I wear pants most of the time, no one has occasion to comment on the size of my knees. I hardly look at them myself except when I shower, and then the issue is whether they're clean, not whether they're overweight. I have opted to continue living in a two-story house as I age, convinced that the extra exercise I get running up and down because I've forgotten what I came down—or up—

for helps keep me healthy. So I want my knees to keep functioning. But *fat*?

Now, my body is not perfect, and its areas of imperfection have increased as I've aged. When I was a young Californian in a time when a not-very-low-cut peasant blouse paired with a knee-length peasant skirt was the extent of provocative female self-display—at least for the girls I was allowed to associate with—I believed that I was poorly built for display, even by those permissive standards. Looking back, I think I was really quite a lovely young woman, albeit small-busted and very long-waisted—as my mother constantly reminded me when she tried to fit me for a homemade dress—but attractive anyway.

And God knows I stood straight. On the posture tests we had to take in junior high gym class, I got A's. We girls walked around the perimeter of the gym with sucked-in tummies, tucked-in butts, and braced shoulders to be judged by the assembled gym teachers and assigned the usual range of grades, mine that reliable A. For reasons I don't now remember, my sister in one of these lineups was once called a "motor moron" by a gym teacher who would assuredly not have school employment in today's more protective times. I don't know whether that name-calling contributed to my sister's aversion to outdoor activity and her passion for dramatic piano playing. It certainly didn't do much for her self-image.

I myself was not an athlete by the standards of my place and time—there were authentic baseball and basketball jocks among Southern California women even then—but I was an athletic person, always strong and in good shape. We had a badminton court in our backyard when I was in high school, where I played with anyone who was available; and my best friend and I used to do "muscle-beach" tricks with each other—one of us on her back, feet raised, balancing the other in horizontal flight. In college I played tennis and swam whenever I could, and I remember long walks from dorm to class or laboratory and back.

My seven years in Manhattan did nothing for my health. And I can remember sitting crouched over my typewriter at *Time* magazine where I spent seven years as a researcher, and having the crane-like head of research come by, run her finger down my spine, and say, "Sit up. Do you want to look like me when you get older?" I certainly did not, and I tried to sit up straight, but my long back always made that a problem. When I sat up to the full length of my upper body, I loomed over whatever I was doing, including eating, causing anyone I was dining with to rear up from their plates, spooked by the sudden disparity in our heights into assuming they had collapsed over the table.

But my early life in Congers, fixing up—with little but paint and energy—a thirteen-room house that Alan and I had bought two years after our marriage, raising two active boys, regularly cutting a half acre of lawn with a push mower, building a rock garden, and the like—reminded me that I was a physical creature; and the move to Piermont in my sixties was definitely a plus in terms of exercise. We had bought a house and garden there that needed lots of work, and after two years of lifting heavy pavers, digging giant hunks of concrete fill out of the soil to prepare our garden beds, moving large evergreens, ripping off plaster and lath and lugging it to the Dumpster, I was, in my young friends' lingo, really buff. The picture on the front cover of a book I published several years later was a true reflection of my state of physical health then. At that time, I could even crouch.

So it was that I arrived at the era of "workouts" and gym memberships for all, conditioned from childhood to view physical activity as part of ordinary life. I remember how amused I was when women were being solemnly assured in the lib literature that it was okay to sweat. This was news? I never went to a gym until several years ago when I briefly attended—mostly out of sociability—a hi-low aerobics class with a friend.

Now that I'm well past "middle" age, people often ask me if I "exercise." I know what they mean by the question, so I tell them that I don't, and that I find intentional exercise readily avoidable. Given the choice, I would much rather spend the day hauling rocks in my garden than going to the gym to do *anything*. So working out is for me a literal description of what I do: I work, and I'm mostly outside when I do it. Everything else—except climbing stairs when I need to reach a different floor, or walking to get where I want to go in the village—seems like artifice, though I know that is a decidedly old-fashioned and minority opinion.

Given that I won't even go to the gym to work on my shape, I find the idea of repairing my body's flaws with surgery breathtakingly offensive. Here is the opening paragraph of the story about fat knees. "Love handles, saddlebags, turkey wattle. Self-conscious women have been trying to reduce those body areas for years. But now with more efficient diets and fitness routines, women are turning to more obscure anatomical zones. The newest worries? 'Bra fat' and 'back fat.'"

Although it's hard to know what could possibly count as a diversion in a rant made up entirely of diversions, I must wander off here to remark on the self-hate involved in those descriptions of ordinary human body parts. In primitive cultures people get old, and when they get old they wrinkle and sag and get wise. And their wisdom is recognized as adding value. And I'll bet you that old women in those cultures don't look at their upper arms and cry.

The story that opens the *Times* article tells of Dana C, a bartender who by her own account has an hourglass figure that attracts whistles as she walks down the street. But atop her blue jeans (her very tight—one assumes—blue jeans), she had a little roll of fat that was "so obvious," according to her, "that her mother constantly came up behind her and pulled her shirt down over it." So for ten thousand dollars she had liposuction on her lower back and then on her upper back, and concluded that it was well worth it. I suppose that depends how much you hate having your mom pull down your shirt.

Enhancing, as the *Times* writer puts it, "the near perfect body parts of the already fit" requires what the writer calls "a designer body" approach that makes use of "precision, selective, or micro liposuction," siphoning out grams of fat from the carefully selected parts that a recent article in the *Journal of Dermatologic Surgery* quoted by the *Times* writer described as "Areas Amenable to Liposuction"—including "buffalo hump" (the upper back), "wings" (bulges around the bra area), the "banana fold" (below the buttocks), "piano legs" (the calves), and, yes, the "chubb," which is the southern term for the kneecap area. Talk about self-hatred . . . and about priorities.

So a medical system that leaves millions of young children uninsured, a medical system that is a major cause of bankruptcy among young families, this system devotes some not insignificant portion of its resources—the 455,000 liposuction operations done last year made it the most popular cosmetic surgery procedure—to ridding anxious females of the fat around their bras, buttocks, and knees.

What I find even more shocking is that a physician director of *bioethics* at a major Manhattan school of medicine is quoted as seeing no problem with all this. I am leaving her nameless out of compassion. "Humans have always been willing," she is quoted as saying, "to invest time, energy and risk in looking attractive, so I don't see smaller lipsosuction procedures as a sign of doom, gloom and the downfall of our culture. *It's just medicine being used to address problems that it could not address before.*" (Italics are mine.)

That is, perhaps, the most depressing news of all. In a time when dread disease ravages millions of people on the planet, when our obsession with an unattainable level of slenderness is causing serious illness among young people, a professor of bioethics sees no need to worry about the fact that "medicine" sees little fatty areas on the body of otherwise fit people as problems properly addressable by surgical intervention.

Which will make micro liposuctionists happy. But of course they are not the only professionals who will benefit from the burgeoning touch-up mentality. The face and neck have long been the most popular targets of personal contempt. And for people who yearn to present an ever-young face to the world, there is Botox. I was skimming some pieces of an old *New York Times* one morning when it was too wet and blowy to go out for that day's paper when my eyes fell on an article in the business section that read "Allergan Makes a Bid for Implant Maker." And there was a picture of a prescription bottle and its box reading BOTULINUM TOXIN TYPE A.

I was a zoology/chemistry major. I was taught that you die of botulinum toxin, one of the deadliest poisons known. So I had to read on to realize that Allergan was the maker of the "anti-wrinkle therapy" Botox, a product whose hype has convinced astonishing numbers of women (and some men) to submit to voluntary injection with a deadly poison in order to temporarily erase the frown creases in their foreheads and the smile lines in their cheeks.

Allergan was bidding for Inamed, a company whose chief attraction appeared to be that its "injectable protein and sugar based cosmetic products" would fit in well with Botox. After the merger, Allergan would have a range of products for facial injection, ranging all the way from sugar to botulinum. (Anyone remember those unsealed canning jars you were urged to throw out to avoid botulism? Apparently some other people remember, too, and opt for sugar.)

But there's more. Inamed also makes the Lap-Band, an "implantable stomach ring" that is considered a less invasive approach than gastric bypass surgery for treating obesity. Oh right, you just make a little hole in the abdomen and put a little ring around the upper part of your stomach and squeeze.

Moreover, the article added, since more than half of Inamed's projected revenue this year came from breast implants, that area of business seemed what the article unsmilingly called "a major growth opportunity."

Clearly the world has arrived at a place that my mother would have found unimaginable, a world in which people are redoing their bodies and faces as if they were home decorating projects! There was nothing that Allergan planned to major in that my mother would ever have heard of or, I suspected, would have wanted to hear of. All she could do was prevent my wearing lipstick until I was nearly an adult and warn me that shaving my legs would make the hair coarse—easy for her to say since she seemed to have been blessed with long black hair that stopped at her scalp line, leaving her with gloriously long hair-free limbs.

And then I remembered. Even my mother could be seduced by the toxin of competitive surgical self-improvement. I was visiting her one day when she was in her nineties, living in a wheelchair in the health facility of a Southern California retirement community with other folks of advanced years, when she said to me that she was thinking of having surgery to raise her sagging right eyelid—a flaw I must confess I had never particularly noticed. Some of the other ladies had done it, and after all her insurance would cover it. At the time I only thought of the ways in which insurance could help confuse necessity and desire, but now I realize that if she were alive today, Mom might not have been as shocked as I was by what Allergan is up to. In fact, she of all people might even encourage me to fix myself up a bit now that I'm single again. I'm happy to say she forgot about her eyelid and when she died some time later was intact.

But even assuming that there is nothing questionable about investing time, money, and medical resources in "touching up" the bad spots, there's always the reupholstered-chair-in-the-living-room problem. Everyone is familiar with the fact that when you bring a new piece of furniture into a room, or add a slipcover to an old couch—everything else looks worse by comparison. It seems inevitable, the face and body being merely bone and flesh, that perfection of one region will reflect badly on other not-so-perfect regions, especially in a beauty contest for which there are no fixed rules. And everyone, suctioned or unsuctioned, will get older and flesh will sag. Hard to imagine that one liposuction or toxin injection will not lead to another, and another, and another, and so on into infinity.

Which brings me back, of course—as almost everything does—to gardening. The great advantage of gardening as a challenge to facial and bodily decay is that even if the body goes, you have something left to love. For working in the garden produces more than exercise; it produces strength, joy, hope, a tan, natural beauty, vegetables, and, in Frances Hodgson Burnett's words, a future. Somehow I can't imagine that having thin knees or perky eyelids can ever provide such rewards.

CHAPTER EIGHT

Things That Break
and Things That Don't

I always pick one achingly cold morning in early winter—as early in these whimsical winters as it turns achingly cold for a day or two—to clean out the old upright freezer that stands in a pantry space just off the kitchen. It is non-self-defrosting. The shelf and door contents are cleared off into plastic milk crates that are lugged out to the terrace, where the freezing weather keeps the contents frozen while I thaw indoors. There are four loads but only three crates so I have to unload one crate onto the glass-topped table out there where the food packages will stay cold as I do the sorting, and then go back for one more fill-up.

Then I come in, put aluminum roasting pans filled with boiling water on the bottom and middle shelves to speed up the thawing and catch the falling ice, turn on the hair dryer and lay it on the middle shelf pointing somewhat up toward the iced-in coils, and head back out dressed for the cold. While the freezer is defrosting, I sort the packages that have been tossed in willy-nilly during the summer, so that I can end up with tomatoes and peppers on one shelf, broccoli, beans, and the like on another shelf—everything identified and, as it is put back in, arranged left to right, back to front on a chart I type up and fasten to the freezer door. This is, of course, one of the tasks that would take less time if two people played, but I have learned to get it done by myself.

Last year an appropriately cold day came early in the season—it was twelve degrees on December 22—and gave me a wonderful head start. The thawing went quickly, and as I wiped down the inside of the freezer to get the last drops of water off, I was suddenly struck by the fact that the walls and shelves, even the coils, everything, looked brand new. This freezer, a Sears Coldspot and a "better," I believe, when Sears listed their appliances as "good," "better," and "best," was bought in July 1971. (Does it seem embarrassingly over-orderly that I found the sales slip in with all the other guarantees for things bought over the years?) This freezer, in perfect shape after nearly four decades, has never been repaired.

I cannot say as much for the "new" appliances Alan and I acquired when we rebuilt our Piermont house, or for the sink ensemble that was also new thirteen years ago. The inside of the freezer door of the expensive new refrigerator was broken several years ago by my older son carelessly replacing a freezer tray. And as for the sink, I have been told by the plumber that he can't get the base of the faucet unscrewed to replace the washer so I will have to replace the whole unit—lever handle, swan-neck faucet, nonworking hose, soap dispenser, and all—in what seems to this environmentally responsible citizen to be a horrendous waste of chrome, among other things. And the stove, ah yes the stove, that's a whole other story—and quite long.

The very first time I laid out cash to repair what was then a five-year-old gas stove, I changed my mind about Maytag. Until that moment, I had been a devoted believer in the brand; years of being amused by ads starring the lonely underutilized Maytag repairman had done their work. So when a Maytag stove—black, handsome, and the right size—appeared before our exhausted eyes at the store where Alan and I were buying appliances, I felt momentarily reassured. Having purchased a house to remodel, we had found ourselves, quite unexpectedly, with a tear-down that required us not only to build a house from scratch, but to fill it up with all the accoutrements of modern life—a necessity that demanded shopping.

I have hated shopping since my infancy, and adulthood has

only sharpened my aversion—perhaps one of the reasons I married a man who loved to shop and went out to do a little of it every day. Consequently, I am a terrible shopper. I am quite incompetent at the thing that most Americans are trained to master—and enjoy—from infancy. Moreover, I think the things I finally buy should last essentially forever. (My Singer sewing machine, bought sometime in the 1950s, has an appropriate lifetime guarantee.) So when Alan and I needed to buy a stove and refrigerator—as well as all the light fixtures, outlet plates, sinks, toilets, shower stalls, newel posts, and the like—while our new home was being constructed, I found the entire experience excruciating.

Since we had to buy a stove, we had high hopes for something dramatically modern but we ended up for $860 with a Maytag slide-in stove, with ordinary burners, not a countertop and separate oven that would have cost $2,000 more. It may have been a reflection of my generally anxious view of life at the time that I wrote in my journal that evening, "I wish I was sure we made the right decision." The fact that we had *not* made the right decision did not become obvious until just after the stove went past its warranty.

Meanwhile, the new stove was installed, and despite some glitches that temporarily threatened its planned location, I was able to happily cook on it, looking out across our vegetable garden to the river as I had planned. After we moved in I became—and far too early—a widow who now had to manage this house Alan and I had built, and its contents . . . on my own. And one day several years after Alan's death, the stove began to beep insistently.

Now, this stove always had a capacity for beeping. It beeps three times when its timer goes off telling you ten or fifteen or thirty minutes have passed; it beeps once to tell you that you can put in your muffins or vegetables for roasting because the oven has reached the temperature you set. And if you asked it to do other tasks for which it is equipped, like cleaning its own oven, I'm sure it would beep to signal that it had completed those.

However, what began in May 1999, less than five years after we and the stove moved in, was not a standard instructional beep. It was an insistent, unceasing beep accompanied by a message on the touch panel —F I—, which seemed to indicate danger—FI what? Was FI-RE implied? Was I risking a fire if I let this go on? I pushed STOP/CLEAR on the touch pad and it stopped—temporarily. Right away I looked in the manual for my Maytag stove to see what —F I— meant. I should note here that I am pretty well organized so I have a set of folders that hold all the guarantees for our various possessions—sorted by room. The instructions for the stove, in the "kitchen" folder, had a separate large-type sheet that answered my questions—sort of.

> Your range is equipped with an electronic control featuring built-in, self-diagnostic software. This software continuously monitors the control to insure safe and proper operation. If the software should detect a questionable situation, a FAULT CODE (F plus a number) will appear in the display and continuous beeps will sound.

The picture that followed showed an F with the number 2. It didn't say what F I meant. Then the instruction went on.

> A fault code indicates that there may be functional error. As a safety precaution the control will automatically cancel the program. Follow the procedures described below to check the range.

What followed was a series of instructions about what to do if the fault code appeared (press the STOP/CLEAR pad and reprogram) when you were using the oven or the self-cleaning cycle, neither of which I was doing. And it warned that you should not use the oven or the self-cleaning cycle again until you have called a repairman. Then it added, "The surface unit can be used."

Well, sure. You could go ahead and cook on the surface unit if you didn't mind having to light the burners with a match or could tolerate the continuous beeping. Furthermore, going ahead and cooking was not what they really wanted you to do because if you went into the manual proper, and were sent to page 24 from a box on page 5 labeled RANGE CONTROL PANEL that mentions the continuous beeping, you would learn that the reappearance of a fault code after you have pressed the CANCEL button means you should "disconnect the power to the range and call a qualified service technician."

If that wasn't an indication that you should be alarmed, I don't know what would be. So I went downstairs to what used to be called the fuse box, and by trial and error found what is now called the circuit breaker that shut off the stove. Then I found the customer assistance number and called, and several days later a certified Maytag repairman came out to repair my stove. Carrying his box of tools and parts, he clumped upstairs, his boots covered with little cloth overshoes, and began to look at the stove.

"What's wrong with it?" I asked him in a seriously frustrated tone of voice. It turned out that the sensors in the touch pad were "compromised." The touch pad, a thin slab of transparent plastic one and a half by four inches in size, had to be peeled off and replaced, a procedure that required removing all the knobs on the touch pad and all the burners on the stove. This activity produced a reaction on the part of the Maytag repairman that encouraged me to amplify my complaint.

I started him off with a few snarly questions like "How can a gas stove need repair? It has tubes that carry gas. What can go wrong? I had a stove for thirty-five years in my other house and it never went bad," and so on. And then he joined me—in a tone so reinforcing to my own indignation that the whole mess began to seem almost worth it.

He was as disgusted as I was. He hated all this unnecessary novelty. "Go to Pennsylvania," he told me "and get a plain stove. This stuff is junk. I'm replacing these things all the time." I had a real Maytag repairman! He wanted to sit in lonely isolation not having to answer calls for sullen plastic touch pads. He was angry enough that he replaced all the burners, which were just about out of warranty, since he was forced to take them off anyway to replace the touch pad—which was, as it happens, just out of warranty. The stove was purchased in October 1994 and it was now May 1999. I was out $143 for a stove that was less than five years old. In thirty years the infrastructure of my old stove never cost a cent.

The warranty on the new touch pad was for a year so the stove didn't start beeping again until shortly after that year had passed. This time I knew what it was going to cost me to call a Maytag repairman, and I tried to change the touch pad's mind. I hit the STOP/CLEAR button forcefully several times in a row, and at first it stopped what seemed semi-permanently, for several days. When punching the touch pad ceased to have much of an effect, I would run downstairs, flip the circuit breaker, and shut it up.

As it happened, turning off the stove circuit also turned off several electrical outlets including the ones the coffee grinder and the toaster were plugged into—and of course it turned off the clock and the burner-igniters on the stove, which meant that I had to use a match whenever I needed to light a burner (on this once automatic stove). And when I wanted to turn on the oven or the broiler, I had to run downstairs, flip the circuit breaker on, and run back up to light the stove or the broiler. And then I had to remember to go down and turn the circuit breaker back off when I shut off the oven or the broiler, because the stove often lay in wait until I had gone to bed and when I got up to use the bathroom in the middle of the night, it would be beeping again!

When I had to turn the circuit breaker back on—to use an outlet, for example—the silence would sometimes go on for a week, or even a month. But the quiet times got shorter and shorter, and eventually I found myself running up and down the stairs with great regularity to turn on the circuit so I could start the broiler, then running down in the middle of eating whatever I had broiled to shut the damn stove up. Although this entire enterprise would obviously have been less stressful had there been a husband to run up and down while I cooked, it really wasn't a satisfactory situation.

Sometimes there were little surprises. One June morning I put a hunk of meat and some vegetables in my Crock-Pot and failed to remember that when I had run down and turned off the stove, I had thereby disabled the outlet into which the Crock-Pot was plugged. So nothing cooked for several hours, and although I finally realized what had happened and plugged the Crock-Pot into a different outlet, I had no meal at dinnertime.

Eventually, of course, I broke down and had the damn thing fixed. It was the end of January 2004, and this time when I called the appliance store to make the appointment, they asked me whether I had a surge protector on the line to the stove. "A surge protector?" I asked, warily. "I doubt it. Why would I?" It turned out that the plastic was sensitive to power surges, so the stove needed a surge protector. "Why didn't they tell me that the last time they fixed it?" I asked as gently as possible. "They didn't know" was the reply. But it got repaired, and for *only* $194.63, to be exact, which brought the post-purchase expense of the stove to just over $330.

Two and a half years later the stove started beeping again—probably just about standard for these touch pads, surge protector be damned. At the time, I had just discovered that my terrace and the rooms under it were rotted ten years after their construction and were going to cost some unthinkable amount to repair. And as I sat there, with my rotting terrace and my beeping stove,

I found myself reflecting lovingly on the hundred-plus-year-old house I had previously lived in for thirty-six years, which never had a speck of rot in it, and of my old Caloric range with its innovative top broiler that worked for thirty years without peeping at all, and I found myself wondering, once again, where we are headed. Things do not really seem to be getting better, unless there is someone out there—a corporation perhaps—who believes that helping keep a Maytag repairman busy is definitely "better."

I couldn't afford a new stove after paying to rebuild the back of my house. And in the year and a half since this one started beeping again, I have been angry enough at Maytag that I haven't fixed it. I've just learned to think of my trips up and down the stairs to flip the switch as added exercise in my old age. I've even trained several people who often have meals with me to go down and do it for me. Sometimes they even ask as they walk in the door, knowing I'm going to be broiling for them, "Do you want me to turn on the stove?" And I have not replaced my sink unit. I have a large laundry-soap jug under the faucet—which actually leaks only a little and only at intervals—and the jug catches any drips, which I then use to rinse out dishes, so I'm probably using less water than I did before I had a drip.

And I have been brought to think of all this at the present moment because my downstairs toilet just started leaking from the joint where the water line meets the tank. (Of course, it's thirteen years old—less than a sixth of my age!) When I discovered it, I turned off the water line, flushed the toilet to empty the tank, mopped the floor, and called a plumber different from the one who said I had to buy a whole new sink unit. But the new plumber hasn't called back yet, so I have been filling gallon jugs with water and pouring them down to flush when necessary. Maybe I'll just let it go.

Given the forecasts for what rising sea levels will do to our Hudson Valley infrastructure—sanitation, utilities, transportation, you name it—a little inconvenience is probably good practice for the future. It isn't everyone who has a working thirty-five-year-old freezer. And I haven't even mentioned my working toaster, the eighty-five-year-old one my parents got for their wedding. I saw a phrase in the paper recently about someone who was "gleefully frugal." I think that hits pretty close to home, and I promise not to gloat when it begins to pay off.

CHAPTER NINE

Potatoes and Escape

Digging potatoes, as I've been doing over the last week or so, is not work, as the word *digging* seems to imply; it's an eagerly awaited pleasure—at least for this grower. At least usually. Last year was an unmitigated disaster potato-wise. After sixteen floods drowned my yard through the year, the potatoes apparently concluded that they might as well dissolve and—as I dug them from the sodden soil—many of them did just that. When I consulted an experienced fellow farmer about what more than just water might have afflicted them, she suggested pink rot or Pythium leak. I opted for Pythium leak, which seemed to have a certain panache, as well as fitting the description of what I had at harvest: The potatoes just collapsed in my hand as I lifted them out of the ground, but they didn't smell rotten—and if I failed to clean up the residue, they dried into a white smear on the brick path.

The total crop turned out to be about thirty-five pounds, give or take a few on which I saw signs of decay after I had weighed them. Since I grow seven different varieties, and since they are intended to last me through the year, that was decidedly not enough, although I made it through the winter thanks to generous farmers I ran across at conferences; hearing of my crop failure, they handed me bags of the ones they hadn't given away during the event.

But this year I'm a winner. I've dug thirty-five pounds already—from a single bed—with two and a half more beds to go. I take some credit for it. There's nothing I can do about clouds emptying on my land, which is a bathtub—higher at the house and river ends of my long lot, and higher too along both sides, the park on the south and my neighbor's property on the north. And the clouds did a lot of emptying here last year. But it's my neighbor's property that accounts for any of my floods that don't descend solely from on high. On nights when the moon is full, the sky clear, and the tide high, his boat ramp invites the Hudson River up, sends it across his yard, under the stockade fence that marks our mutual property line, and down into my bathtub just waiting to fill with water.

So one spring—confident that sixteen floods in a single year were a meaningful hint from Mother Nature—I paid to have a wall constructed. Eighteen inches in from that leaky fence, a former wrestling coach named Dave built me a beautiful rock wall a foot and a half high and lined with black plastic, a sort of giant planter designed to hold back the water and let it puddle in my neighbor's yard. And as far as I know, it's worked. I've been slightly flooded twice, once when we had five and a half inches of rain in three hours and everything around me was also flooded, and another time when we had three and a half inches in even less time.

But leaving aside these extraordinary outbursts, we've had really perfect growing weather this season, a genuine spring for the first time in years, and a summer in which most of the rains have come at the right times with lots of sunshine between. So I had high hopes for the potatoes, and couldn't wait for the vigorous plants to die back so I could begin to dig.

With tomatoes and peppers, you know whether you're likely or not to harvest a crop almost from the time the first blossom opens and the first tiny pepper or tomato sets. You can watch it happen. It's not like that with potatoes. You plant the seed potatoes, wait for the shoots to emerge—an interminable wait if you've put them in cold ground—and then watch them rapidly grow into lusty five-foot-high plants, topped eventually with nodding clusters of lovely five-sided pink, lilac, or white flowers, which I've been told is a signal that they're setting tubers.

A few weeks later the plants begin to die. That's when non-gardening visitors to your flourishing midsummer garden turn away without comment from the beds with the sick-looking plants, assuming you'd rather not discuss your failures. The foliage of early potatoes dies down earliest—a nice demonstration of consistency—while the foliage of the durable Purple Peruvians seems determined not to give up until frost; I often need to dig those lumpy dark tubers when the foliage is still green if I'm to get them indoors before the ground freezes.

This is how it goes. You put the spading fork into the soil near the brown remnants of the plant—by now just stems—pull back on the handle and, Mother Nature willing, you will glimpse the rounded sides of a cluster of potatoes, beige, netted brown, red, white, yellow, or the almost invisibly dark Purple Peruvians. So you kneel down and begin to grub them out, one after the other after the other, until your harvest bucket is almost full.

Potatoes provide one of the delightfully nondemanding harvests from a subsistence mini farm—unlike the tomato glut that's welcome but insistent on its own timing. Onions and garlic are other patient crops. Dig potatoes into a bucket and they'll just sit there until you're ready to deal with them. Dig garlic or pull onions, strew them about where they can dry, and—if you keep them out of the rain—you can wait to braid the onions or tie up the bunches of garlic until a nice sunny but cool day when you'd like to sit on the porch and reflect. On the other hand, when you pick tomatoes, or when you don't pick them for that matter, you either deal with them promptly or they rot in your face in the company of a swarm of fruit flies.

I allow special friends to help me dig potatoes, and they almost always fall into the same addictive grubbing that afflicts me as I plunge in my hands to find the last tuber in a bed. It's like a child's dream (or at least *this* child's dream) of walking along and suddenly spotting a nickel on the side of the road (a nickel was a lot in the Great Depression). As you stoop to pick it up, you see another coin under it, and then another, until you have a handful of change. Potatoes are like that. They seem like a gift; in fact, the potato growers association has come up with a message about their crop that seems to me much more worthy of a public relations prize than slogans like "Got Milk?": It's "Potatoes . . . Goodness Unearthed." They are. And they feed you through the winter.

I try to unearth each variety of potato fairly promptly, since no more potatoes will be produced once the foliage has disappeared and I have burrowing insects underground that enjoy tasting the crop before I do if it's left buried. However, if you trust the local micro fauna, you can leave potatoes in the ground until late fall and dig them all at once.

Should one choose to accept the offer, potatoes, onions, and other storage vegetables offer the gardener a rare opportunity: midseason escape. Go away when the tomatoes are frantically converting carbon dioxide, air, and water into leafy tissue that reaches up and out trying to take over the territory, and you come home to a mess that takes so much cleaning up it's hardly worth it. So I tend to spend summers at home.

And this is fine with me. In fact, I think everyone should stay home more, try to make the places they are living—are forced sometimes to live—livable. If the planet is to remain inhabitable, we can't give up on the homes and communities we live in, but must turn them into places where our hearts rejoice. I think it was the western writer Wallace Stegner who said that every second home is a testament to the failure of the first.

It was a Sunday morning in the middle of a Memorial Day weekend when I found myself in the garden thinking about all those people in their cars driving to get somewhere they thought they wanted to be for the weekend. A recent National Public Radio piece on road trips had described these weekend hegiras as a testimony to hope. You hope that you'll find just what you're looking for, that you'll stop at some scenic overlook, get out and photograph it, and it will do what? Change your life? The reality is that the kids are restless in the backseat; you can't get the temperature right in the front seat; you're usually stuck in traffic much more than once; and no one will really want to look at your photos when you get back.

It's probably clear by now how much of my home and how many of my pleasures are centered in my garden, which is not so much large—a thirty-six-foot-wide village lot—as complex, and often quite beautiful. On either side of a five-foot-wide path, it holds eleven yard-wide beds, mostly planted to vegetables and separated by two-foot paved walks. The main path is planted to clover and runs down the center of the garden to a grassy bank bordered with shrubs and flowers that edges the river. And it's there sitting on the riverbank pulling weeds that I have often found myself thinking about my fellow citizens' ceaseless travel, after which I chide myself for feeling judgmental about other people's search for *pleasure*. After all, as someone once reminded me following one of my self-righteous rants, those people are looking for pleasure after a week or a month or a year of working at a job they hate. My problem, I realized then, was not the pleasure, but the search. Specifically, I am unhappy about the impact of all that travel.

Since our restlessness is seriously accelerating the trashing of the earth, it seems at least useful to question our incessant movement to other places. Done aloud, such questioning is usually, alas, the beginning of a tricky exchange, like the one I had some time ago with a fellow community gardener who inquired about a recent trip of mine. What with one thing and another I ended up telling her that I had trouble just "traveling" because it used up so many resources. I have worried a lot about planetary warming ever since Senator Al Gore first held hearings about it in the late 1970s. And as I told my fellow gardener, I've not been comfortable traveling since I read somewhere that if we humans shared equally the CO_2 pollution the earth can tolerate, each of us would be allowed one flight to Europe—in our lifetimes. I don't think that's accurate, but it's close enough to truth to be thought provoking—and alarming. It turns out that there's a lot more to worry about than long lines at airports, people exploding their shoes, or sick air in the passenger cabin.

She looked shocked—as if I had just said something vulgar. She said she loved to travel, and just felt lucky to have enough money and time to enjoy herself and do all the things she enjoyed doing. At some point she added that she hadn't been aware of the problems I was describing, and didn't think she wanted to be. "Well," I said, "I can't help it. I already know about them."

I've avoided writing about travel in the past not just because being footloose is so American, or because moving us around is such a major industry, but because—sitting on my riverbank—I know it's not normal to live in a place where the view makes you draw a startled breath of pleasure. At a minimum, one runs the risk of seeming insensitive. "Oh, sure, you don't need to travel; why would you when you live in paradise?"

I couldn't figure out how to answer that until I was reflecting one morning on what was at the time a relatively recent addition to *The New York Times,* a section called Escapes—recently killed by the economic meltdown—that celebrated wonderful places to run off to. The prices at some of these destinations suggested that the target escapees included some of the richest people in the world; the *Times* editors had concluded, I guess, that the paper's well-to-do readers would like to learn about places where they could get away from it all. So those who least need to get away because they have the most choices about where and how to live are doing much of the escaping. Given that fact, and my own contentment, I feel perfectly justified in asking why someone much richer than me needs to escape from her Long Island McMansion with its tennis courts, its swimming pool, and its ocean view.

Which is when I understood why my conviction that people

ought to stay home more was not unfair. For my lack of sympathy for the restlessness of the über-wealthy among us is exceeded by my empathy for the billions more families living in urban or rural slums, people who really deserve a chance to escape to one of those island paradises—unlikely as it is that their dream will be realized.

And it is some of these folks for whom escape seems impossible who have begun to teach our imploding cultures how we might brighten the corners where we live. In cities worldwide it is the slum dwellers, the people living in the poorest parts of the most chaotic urban agglomerations, who have taken hold of and transformed pieces of their neighborhoods, often against great odds, into community spaces that help feed them, small paradises where children play, retired men work among the vegetables, and residents come together for festivals. In much of the world, these are neighborhoods that, outside the confines of these community gardens, are grim beyond the experience of most of us.

The wisdom these "escapees" bring us from the edges of our known world is that we will never salvage a habitable planet if we don't try to make the places we live into the places we want to be; we can't create livable communities if we spend much of our time dreaming about escaping to somewhere else. An acquaintance here in my village who lives in a luxurious apartment with a gorgeous view once told me delightedly that he and his wife were going on their second safari. It will be great to "get away from it all," he said. I could only speculate that the "all" they were getting away from was their life.

Transporting us to remote "destinations" and making them exotic and luxurious enough to satisfy our inner sybarite devours resources, not least fossil fuels, whose burning raises the CO_2 level of the atmosphere and causes parts of the planet to warm. The warming planet accelerates the melting of the polar ice sheets, thus threatening murres, and seals, and penguins, and polar bears by distancing them from their food. The destination beaches we fly to and the island nations to which we escape are all threatened by the rise of the seas due to warmer water and ice melt, consequences of the warming caused by fossil fuel combustion to which we fewer than 5 percent of the planet's population contribute more than 25 percent of the global total, a substantial proportion of which is produced by our consuming 43 percent of the world's gasoline.

How's this for a story with a moral? One summer morning in 2001 *The New York Times,* which is, as must by now be obvious, my newspaper of record, printed a story headlined "Penguins in Trouble World-Wide" about the potential disappearance of the Magellanic penguins from the South Pole region. Global warming was melting the ice on which they lived. Later in the day I e-mailed a farmer friend in Wisconsin:

> I had an Aha! today when I saw in the paper that the penguins are disappearing. My first thought was "Oh, God, I've got to go see them before they disappear." My second thought was, "It's that sort of impulse that is helping them disappear." If we all travel all the time to see things before they're gone, we're helping warm the planet, which means they will be gone. We've gotten used to thinking that because we can do everything technically, we also can do it, so we go . . . on and on.

A day or so later the *Times* published, presumably without irony, a letter from a man named Joel who commented on the awe he and his wife felt when they went to Punta Tombo, Argentina, in 1997 and walked among the Magellanic penguins. "We rated this day as being as awesome as standing on China's Great Wall and visiting the Nile Valley. Anyone who goes to Argentina should make this visit. It is tragic to read of the penguins' hardship."

The penguins' *hardship,* Joel? They're going to die. But go ahead, take that jet, burn that fuel, go see the penguins and speed their demise before someone else does. It'll help keep the economy going. Joel and his wife are, alas, not alone. "The Race to Alaska Before It Melts" is the headline in a much more recent *Times* travel story. Travel and tourism is, after all, the largest industry in the world—worth $1.2 trillion in the United States alone—and responsible for one in every twelve jobs.

Which means that when I question the chronic urge to travel, I am not only criticizing my fellow citizens' choice of recreation, I'm undermining the global economy. This includes the economies of poor countries where tourism represents the second largest source of foreign exchange after oil. Since the number one reason for travel is reported to be shopping, and I'm also opposed to the endless consumption shopping supports, railing against travel makes me seem even more churlish than usual.

However, our restlessness not only inevitably destroys the beauty we are traveling to look at, it also destroys the very cultures that make these places different enough to provide an un-home-like experience. The four million tourists who saw Tibet in 2007 far outnumbered the resident population.[13] It was in a review of a book called *The Native Tourist*[14] that I found the most indignant layout of the problems tourists cause when governments focused on marketing their nation to tourists evict "existing communities from coastal areas, forests and national parks for the sake of five-star hotels," reducing the indigenous people to "custodians of trinket-stalls or security guards for second homes locked up for much of the year."

I myself have seen, alas, what the reviewers call "embalmed cultural rituals" where a fake Mayan football game is regularly played in costume for tourist amusement—without, of course, the culturally appropriate death of the winners that would have followed in ancient times.

The reviewer of this book is outraged by the fact that its authors do not see this as a moral issue but as just another academic discipline that needs research. What possible good can research do, they ask, "to stem the frenzied mobility brought to 'developing' countries by . . . the Western way of wealth." Across the world tourism has ruined destinations without providing significant reward to the peoples who live there. "How shall we reclaim," the authors ask, "purposeful and significant journeys to the places where others live from the brutal invasiveness of industrialized travel?"

How indeed?

So there you have it. I can't help feeling uncomfortable about just moving around, and I'm certain my uneasiness has not contributed to my friends' anticipation of their next trip—or my next visit. So I'm happy to know at least that I am not alone in my worry about our footloose way of life in the teeth of our present global crises. When poet Gary Snyder was asked what one could do to help save the planet, his answer was, "Stay put." One of the virtues of being committed to feeding oneself from a garden, as I said way back when I was digging potatoes, is that it tends to make you happy doing just that.

CHAPTER TEN

If My Parents Had
Danced in the Supermarket

If my parents had danced in the supermarket, I might have been Judy Collins or Mary of Peter, Paul, and Mary. If my parents had danced in the supermarket, I might have had music weaving through and through my life. But they didn't, and I haven't. What provoked this cascade of thinking was a radio interview I caught midway in which a Latin musician described his parents as such a loving pair that they danced at a moment's notice— even while waiting in the supermarket line. At that moment, my whole history rather than passing quietly before my eyes, came crashing down on my head, and the recognition overwhelmed me: It's all right there, I said. I am what I am partly because my parents did not, would not, and indeed could not have *imagined* dancing in the supermarket.

And what flooded my mind then was not what I might have been, but what I was, and how the life flow down through the family had led me to where I was today, duty-ridden, swamped by paper, feeling a chronic responsibility to the planet, more than desirably perfectionistic, and cursed, or blessed, with an ironic sense of humor that is sometimes—indeed too often—misunderstood. (Which is why I smile to remember that at the end of one semester my students suggested I should do environmental stand-up comedy.)

There was my mother, Joyce Fisher, youngest child in a poor family of Dutch extraction—Dutch *Reformed* extraction, an important distinction—living in a two-thousand-person northwest Iowa town named Orange City in which seven churches vied for piety. And my father, Chester Harlan Dye, who grew up several hundred miles south of her in an even smaller Iowa town named Carson. He was the youngest child in a large family with an ailing mother and lots of dominating sisters, and—so family myth has it—he moved out of his house to the riverbank to escape all those women when he was twelve. Chet was always clever with his hands. He could do anything, and ultimately did, from building houses, to setting toilets, to wiring the Venice pier when he came to California newly discharged after World War I from brief landlocked service in the navy.

My mother landed in California because her much older sister was being courted by a fine widower, fifteen years her junior. Aunt Nell must have been by then in her thirties, a handsome settled maiden lady, and ineligibly old, in judgmental Dutch Reformed eyes, to marry such a young man. But he was persistent, so she fled to California, taking with her my very willing mother—then in her early twenties and desperate to escape church-ridden little Orange City. Southern California was thick with Iowans in those days—so thick that the "Iowa picnic," held every year at Long Beach, was divided up by counties and one could find there former neighbors newly arrived in the promised land. Aunt Nell's suitor found her in California and took her back home to live happily in sophisticated Des Moines until my beloved uncle Fritz died, after which she moved back to California, where she outlived him by fifteen years.

Ultimately my parents met in California, probably not at an Iowa picnic, but surely in an Iowa context. And I suspect they never danced—in the supermarket or anywhere else. Unquestionably the times put a damper on dancing. They married in 1925 and managed to have only two girls before the Great Depression struck. My mother, one of six, had wanted a big family, my father surely wanted at least one boy, but they were both cautious people, and in the 1930s caution was everyone's operative mode.

I can imagine people who would have danced through the

Depression (dancing is free after all), but I can't imagine my father dancing even in the Jazz Age when Dad and Mom met. I think of my stiff, unemotional father, who could never tell my beautiful mother whom he adored that he saw her beauty. It's impossible to think of him moving even clumsily on a dance floor with her in his arms.

I think of the charcoal sketch of my father's grandfather that I have on my wall; it bears that unforgiving Dye family face. And I remember the stern (though often amused) face of my mother's oldest sister, my aunt Cora, and see all that repression pushing down through the decades, meeting with little resistance in my stiff father, tyrannizing my instinctively loving mother for years. She never really broke free, though she wore pants long before the other ladies did, and stopped going to church in her old age, saying that she felt more religious just listening to Nature—and she whistled a lot while she did housework.

Many of my father's nieces and nephews ended up in California, and I can remember the wives of the Dye spawn calling my mother in tears about their husbands' apparent lack of feeling for them. And I remember my mother reassuring them that the Dye men, while never demonstrative, *were* faithful.

My mother might have danced had she not married Dad. She had a choice, she once told me. Two men wanted to marry her, and she asked her wise older sister whom she should choose. Nell's reply was often repeated by my mother when she was trying to convince us that my father was really a man to be loved even when he seemed to my sister and me to be not very lovable.

"If you marry Jerry," Nell said to my mom, "if he gets a little extra money he'll buy himself a new hat. If you marry Chet, when he gets a little money, he'll buy *you* a new hat." It was the Depression. Mom opted for Chet, the conservative choice. And Nell was right. My father was always selfless with money; he had so much insurance for his family that my mother lived better after he died. It was only his emotions with which he was stingy.

I suspect that whatever he knew about sex was pretty unsophisticated and what my mom knew—and conveyed to me—was little more than that it was the way to make babies, and "men need it more." Looking back now at who she really was, I suspect that had she married the other man who was courting her at the time, she would have had a better chance of having more than that to say about sex—and she surely would have had more dancing.

So what is the curve of my life? A happy infant, surely a happy infant. Pictures of me as a baby are uniformly smiling; pictures of my older sister, Barbara—who undoubtedly resented my arrival—consistently show her looking rather sad or disappointed. Much later my mother told me that Barbara could never be pleased. Whatever she got was never good enough, so I'm sure my mother experienced my arrival with a different temperament as a pleasant surprise. I remember happily climbing into the laps of visitors when I was an infant, much to my sister's deep embarrassment and distress.

My parents worried a lot about their daughters growing up to be "fine young women," which meant, of course, honest, clean, obedient—and proper. My engineer father believed children needed to be trained—like puppies, but fortunately he was at work a lot of the time. And when he was home—out in his garage-shop making something—he didn't like to be disturbed, although he would show off his accomplishment proudly when it was done.

My mother had her Dutch upbringing to contend with, and when we went back to Orange City, Iowa, for visits we all got it full in the face. I remember the breathlessly hot Iowa Sunday morning when Barbara and I were just three and five. We toddled downstairs dressed in shorts and Aunt Cora sniffed in shock, "Joyce, it's *Sunday!*" And we were taken back upstairs to be properly dressed. For us it was a novelty; for my mother it was her upbringing. But back home she did her best to apply it gently. So

I grew up with guilt, guilt—and a chronic anxiety about stepping out of line.

I also grew up with a chronic sense of obligation toward what seemed to be a world of unfortunates out there, despite the fact that the only time our family was relatively well off was during the Great Depression when my father—a civil service employee—had a job. During World War II when I was in my teens, my mother was always packing up clothes we had hardly finished wearing (and our wardrobes were not bountiful) to send to the beleaguered citizens of Holland.

As for money, my sister and I each saved something for Christmas (probably a nickel) every month from our tiny allowances, thus collecting a relative fortune by the holidays, which we doled out at the local five-and-dime buying presents for friends and family. Then came the unforgettable Christmas when my sister and I, having saved a few pence from this tiny allotment, managed to buy a twelve-inch-high Christmas tree and a single string of lights. We set it up in our playroom and I spread a layer of cotton beneath it, made tiny skating figures out of pipe cleaners, and set them up on a lake made from a mirror. When it was all done, my mother came up to admire it. Then she said wouldn't it be nice if we gave it to an old lady shut-in who lived behind us, the mother of neighbors we liked. I hardly knew the old lady; my mother didn't even like her. But we gave it anyway. Certainly giving it away was better than feeling guilty!

Because when my mother was really disappointed in something we had done—like my sister throwing her cup on the floor instead of drinking from it at the age of one as the baby book said she should—she cried. She cried at me right through college, when she found my roommate's cigarettes and thought I had started smoking. And of course smoking implied other major sins. And I so wanted to please her—because she was a loving mother with a glorious sense of humor despite everything—that

I tried always to do the right thing. And felt intolerably guilty when I couldn't—or didn't.

Luckily I seem to have inherited much of what my mother wanted to be. She told me almost guiltily, when she felt sure it was too late to ruin me, that I had really gotten the best of both of my parents. I had my mother's loving temperament and humor, she said, and my father's engineering mind. I loved my mother's mind as I didn't love my father's—and I think I have finally grown into some of it; I am surely grateful to have inhaled her enthusiasm for gardening. But unquestionably, I was raised by people who couldn't have danced in the supermarket, and looking back I can see now what a difference that made.

CHAPTER ELEVEN

Watery Lessons

One night in class—trying to explain to my students just what purpose agriculture served in our society—I had to take up the issue of taxpayer supports to farmers. Normally referred to as subsidies, these range from direct payments to compensate grain and soybean producers for low market prices, to the bargain-priced California water awarded to California's giant agribusinesses. These subsidies help explain why we have what we call "cheap food" in the supermarket. What we really have are cheap raw materials like corn, soy, and wheat, of which the true costs of raising are paid on our tax bills. Feeders and processors transmute these into cheap beef, pork, and chicken and the thousands of processed food and drink products that clutter the supermarket shelves. Most of the profit from these objects is then returned to people who didn't grow the "raw materials" in the first place. Many of us believe these subsidies are misdirected, that they should be used, if at all, to insure family farmers against losses and to help support conservation and other good things we need.

The underlying question, of course, is: Why should government support farmers at all? Why can't agriculture simply compete in what we like to call the free market like other industries—carriage making, for example, which died out abruptly when the demand for it disappeared? The immediately obvious answer is that we cannot allow the market for food to die out without much of the human race dying out as well. Most of us are ill equipped to feed ourselves from the earth. If we're going to eat, we need to have food available to buy, and someone somewhere needs to grow it.

That means there's an inevitable market for food producers to sell into—indeed, it's an increasing market since the population of the world keeps growing. So—and this is the second question—why should we have to prop up our farmers? If food producers in this country can't survive in the face of the "free market," why don't we just let people in other countries grow food for us while we take on better-paying jobs?

Such a startling (and startlingly final) solution to our farm problem has been implied often and proposed from time to time, most bluntly perhaps by an economist named Steven C. Blank who once wrote a book called *The End of Agriculture in the American Portfolio.* This odd treatise assured us that even if "foreigners" grew all our food we could still have Big Macs by importing wheat from Canada and beef from Argentina. Since agriculture seems not to be profitable enough to allow most of our farmers to survive, Blank suggested, why shouldn't we just let someone else produce our food and buy it from them?

The answer to this second question is almost as obvious as the answer to the first: We live in a world in which it is neither attractive nor safe to imagine that we might be held hostage by our need for imported food as we have been held hostage by our need for imported oil. Which means that we need somehow to go on producing food where we live. And we must find some way to guarantee that the people who now produce it can continue to do so without sacrificing their families and their futures to do so.

Now, the question of why our farmers can't make money in a "free market" that is neither free nor a real market is beyond the scope of what I hope to say in this chapter, but the larger question of what makes agriculture different, the reason why we need to find some way to insure farmers—as opposed to steelworkers or store clerks—against disaster, is fundamental. Agriculture is uniquely vulnerable to the natural world—especially to the weather—in a way that no other industry is, a fact of which I am repeatedly reminded because of my own efforts to grow food.

My financial vulnerability is obviously trivial compared with that of real farmers who depend for their livelihood on what they can produce. However—because of my peculiar location—I am more vulnerable to the elements than most farmers who would not choose a place as soggy as mine to farm in.

But as I have written before, I carry on growing food in my own backyard to remind me—and those I teach—of farmers' vulnerability and therefore the vulnerability of all of us to Nature. And as global warming increases the instability of our climate, the lessons I've had to learn personally are becoming more frequent and more urgent.

My garden floods. It has always flooded, and despite a number of mitigating measures I have taken—building a stone wall backed by impermeable plastic to prevent the neighbors' overflow into my yard at high tide, raising all the beds over time, and so on—the flooding is getting worse. But it was not until 2005— when I experienced my third major flood in a single year and October repeatedly broke existing all-time records for rainfall— that I finally acknowledged that it was time for me to grow up.

Between my second and third floods, New Orleans and much of the Gulf Coast were washed out, and Central America was once again devastated by mudslides. Indeed, as Wilma—the last hurricane to have a name that year because they finished running through the alphabet and ran out of letters—crossed the Yucatán, it sat long enough over the tourist island of Isla Mujeres to drop five feet of rain in twenty-four hours.[15] I find I am unable—and surely unwilling—to imagine how five feet of rain can fall that fast.

Two months later[16] Afghanistan felt the full impact of Nature twitching her rocky skin, global twitching that is now forecast to be more frequent as the frozen poles of the planet shed their weighty overlayers of ice in response to greenhouse warming.[17] Compared with catastrophes like those, anything that happens to my backyard farm is embarrassingly trivial. It is my place and

I love it, and its repeated dunking grieves me; but in the third trimester of my life, I am trying hard to pay close attention so as to extract the meaning of what happens to my tiny piece of the planet.

So it was the early flood of 2005 that taught me my first lesson for that year.

> APRIL 1—It rained last Saturday, and rained, and rained
> . . . and rained—and my backyard went deeply underwa-
> ter . . . Saturday was not the first time my backyard had
> flooded from a heavy rain. It was not even the first time
> *that week.* Monday we had endured a storm that dropped
> 4–5 inches of water starting in the middle of the night;
> by the middle of the next day I had a backyard under so
> much water that it took two days to go down. And down
> is the only way the water can go. There's no draining *out*
> since my yard has higher land around it on all sides. It
> was only Thursday that the soil dried out enough to allow
> me to walk out there without sinking into the muck.
>
> So I was, to put it mildly, profoundly grieved to see a
> second flood in the same week. When I woke Saturday
> morning, the yard was already going under—I had antic-
> ipated that, and told a friend who planned to come work
> (indoors) with me by late afternoon that she probably
> wouldn't arrive in time for the excitement of watching
> the yard flood. Keeping one's sense of humor is essential.
> As I forecast, she didn't make it. By the time she arrived,
> in a heavy rain, I was in deep despair about another week
> without gardening.
>
> She told me to stop looking out the window, insisted
> that I sit at dinner with my chair facing away from the
> garden, and urged me to remember when I got up in
> the morning that I should not put up the blinds in my
> bedroom. My mood *was* much better by the time night

fell. We watched an old movie, remembered when times were simpler, and went to bed in our respective rooms. And as I fell asleep, I tried not to hear the little noises that indicated the rain was continuing to fall. The nation lost an hour that night, springing forward for Daylight Saving Time, and when I got up, I *didn't* put up the bedroom blinds.

I couldn't, alas, avoid for long going to the second floor kitchen–dining room where there are no window coverings. What greeted me as I looked out on my "garden" was a 36-foot-wide, 100-foot-long lake unbroken by any paths or borders, that ran from close to the house—at the level of the toolshed floor up to and slightly over the elevated riverbank. That meant there were at least twelve inches of water over the entire yard. And it was still raining, though more gently—you could see drops on the surface of my lake where the cloudy sky was reflected.

I tried hard to behave as an adult. My friend had come in a car which she had, fortunately, left in front of the house; the parking lot where she would otherwise have left her car was filled with enough water to cover the floorboards of anything parked there. My own car was stranded on the near side of that lake, so Toni drove us down to get a ritual Sunday morning bacon and egg sandwich for each of us and we came home to eat it— with me once again sitting so as to face away from the garden. (To readers who are offended by my Sunday breakfast: I have come to consider it more important to provide once-a-week support to the lovely storekeepers who sell the sandwich in question than to live undeviatingly by my "local meat only" principles.) As we ate, I gamely tried to keep in mind how much worse it was for the people in New Jersey whose homes were flooded. I

confess that thinking about their misery did not eliminate mine. I was desolate.

My friend left, and I went down to make some phone
calls. I had by this time opened the blinds in my office—
which I had closed earlier to prevent myself from seeing
the havoc in the garden. And as I was sitting talking
on the phone I suddenly saw something unexpected.
I looked hard. A pair of mallards was swimming in my
yard. I burst out laughing and told my caller about it. She
said I should put the story on one of my chatty telephone
messages and when we hung up, I did. But I couldn't stop
watching the mallards. Somehow focusing on their pres-
ence atop the water that filled my yard made the whole
mess tolerable. I fell in love with them on the spot.

The ducks paddled up and down the garden paths,
ducking their heads into the water, to eat an occasional
unwary floating worm I assumed, and finally the male
climbed on top of something down at the foot of the
garden where there is a very low concrete pad with
a rough fireplace where I roast peppers during the
summer. At first I thought the handsome potential father
was sitting on the plastic bag of kindling I have there,
but then I looked closely. I had cut down the foliage of a
big clump of Dutch iris and laid them on the bed next to
the fire area. A premade nest. "Paradise" the ducks must
have concluded. Here was this wonderful pond rich with
insect life and underwater clover paths, and piles of dead
reeds perfect for nesting. "Where could it all have come
from?" they must have asked themselves.

Even if I had wanted to, I couldn't have gotten out
there to warn them that all this was temporary, and I
had no desire to share that information. Just like any
overanxious grandmother, I had already planned their
future. I saw them taking advantage of this ready-made

nest to lay eggs immediately, though my plans for the eggs were not exactly grandmotherly. I told myself that the little ones would discover themselves stranded on dry land, so it would be kinder if I just ate the eggs. Local food.

All this thought, you understand, was the product of a few hours of intermittently watching those lovely birds enjoy themselves in my underwater garden. Meanwhile, the rain had stopped and the water had begun to go down. As it began to get dark—late because we were now on Daylight Saving Time—I looked out and found myself concerned that the ducks had left because the water was shallowing. No, there they were, exploring the paths on the south side of the garden. I worried a little that the water was going down too fast. And it did. Next morning the lake and the ducks were gone. And I had learned something about love triumphing over self-pity.

I don't think the ducks have visited since. If nesting was their intention, they've already done that somewhere else, and if they came back, they came in my absence. I was away when Nature next made clear that she was not through for the year. And this time the lesson she taught was different.

The summer's second flood led me to label this as the year of "small potatoes," a phrase that my *Dictionary of Americanisms* defines as "A person or thing regarded as trivial, insignificant, paltry, etc." At the time I chose the name, I realized that disparaging something by calling it "small potatoes"—an insignificant product of agriculture—seemed very American. Older cultures have a kind of enduring reverence for things that come out of the soil. But we've been a nation of bigness and uniformity fans with the result that we can now have, for much of the year, utterly tasteless strawberries, hard and white in their centers but the size of golf balls.

The potatoes I grow are sometimes small, but come in remarkably different colors and sizes, uniformity being quite unnatural. I unearth many tubers much smaller than any you ever see in the market, and in a good year I tend to let pinkie-nail-sized ones wash out of the bucket when I rinse the heaviest dirt off the harvest. The inch-long ones I usually store—all the varieties jumbled together—in a shoe box that I have labeled TINY TATERS, in private mocking reference to the objects that carry that label in the supermarket freezer case.

Early in the season, I serve tiny taters—which come in red, white, and blue—to guests willing to be surprised at the table. Putting a mess of little patriotic potatoes on someone's plate wins you credit as a memorable host, especially to guests familiar with your skeptical view of what too often passes for patriotism. By fall, when the August overwhelm has passed, I tend to forget the TINY TATERS box. When I remember them again later in the year, they have usually begun to sprout—which all stored potatoes will do, shrinking a little as they do so. And these little balls of flesh are so small, there's not much left to eat once they've shrunk, so they often get thrown out.

But this was the year when *nothing* would get thrown out. This was eating-tiny-tater season, in fact it was eating-teeny-weeny-potato season because the fourteen inches of muddy water that poured into my yard at the end of June did more damage to my vegetables than any preceding aqueous experience I'd had as a riverside dweller. Although I missed the excitement as it was happening, I'm pretty certain that *this* water all came down from the mountainside rather than up from the sometimes bumptious Hudson River that runs by my garden, and it was the consequence of a downpour of biblical proportions combined with stupid human overbuilding.

The flood began by washing water and rocks from the top of the famous Hudson Palisades where there had been too much careless land clearing and construction. Then—gaining force, mud, and rocks—the water cascaded down the mountain, clogging the storm drains with boulders as it came. I'm at the bottom of the hill, and have no idea what I would have done if I had been forced to watch the disaster occur. As it is, when I came home, I walked out into a garden coated with mud twelve to fourteen inches up the stems of whatever plants were still living.

But much of the garden was not living. All the brightly blooming annuals were gone. Well, not gone, exactly; they were corpses, covered with mud and lying there in a gray-brown desolation. In one bed where zucchini was just humping out of the ground when I left, three small mud-covered disks were all that was visible. The next day I learned a new word for beets. As I was told by Octavio, whom I hired to help me clean up my yard, they are called *remolatcha* in Spanish. But his first word, as he walked through surveying what he was to do, was *"Muerte."* (Later I brought him back to show him that the beans that he declared *muerte,* or dead, had survived and begun, very belatedly, to bear.)

Octavio was using a fine spray to get the mud off the leaves, so I let him clean off only some of the plants—the last thing they needed was more water. After he sprayed down some of the evergreens and vegetables, I used a soft round brush to clean the dried mud off others, including the beets. It was all pretty sad.

Overall, it proved to be an interesting experiment—if you like that sort of thing—in discovering what was and what wasn't bothered by being covered with mud. The raspberries sent a mixed message. The early-summer bearers seemed relatively unfazed, yet I lost all but two of the fall heritage plants I had started just a year earlier after watching a flourishing raspberry bed succumb to another flood. Half the tomato plants died—all but two in one bed, only one in another, leaving no information on what distinguished the survivors from the victims at the same elevation no more than fifteen feet away.

The brassicas—broccoli, brussels sprouts, kale, and the like—seemed undaunted. I merely brushed the caked mud off their leaves with a paintbrush, and they went on producing prolifically into winter. Amazingly enough some of the plants most notoriously tender in the spring, the peppers and eggplants, pretended they hadn't even noticed their near-death by drowning.

The potato plants, which had obviously been entirely submerged, were full of resentment and mud. They either gave up the ghost immediately or within a week, although some of the early varieties may have been intending to die back anyway as potatoes do when they have finished setting tubers. I don't think the russets had planned to give up so soon, though; when their foliage died back, I had to dig them all and they were abundant but half-sized.

Only one potato variety managed to look utterly unfazed, standing up green and lively, and two weeks later heedlessly clambering over the front of the bed in which it was planted, covering up the space formerly occupied by a less vigorous companion. The survivor was Purple Peruvian, descendant of a variety grown by the natives of Peru, people who lived so close to the margin that they didn't waste their time growing crops that couldn't stand up to a little pain.

I have noticed the aggressive vigor of Purple Peruvian before, but since defiance of drowning seemed a characteristic unlikely to favor a *mountain* potato, this performance was especially awe inspiring. It also provided a forceful lesson—in a year when I wondered if I would have to get through winter without potatoes—of the importance of biological diversity.

And this year I didn't let the pinkie-nail-sized potatoes wash out of the pail; I was desperate. I knew they wouldn't store at all, so I began immediately serving them to anyone who would sit still and eat. I sloshed them around in water to clean them, and then steamed them for about ten minutes and applied butter. They were a sensation. Not only were they something you could only eat when you visited me, they had a very special quality because of the ratio of skin to mealy interior. They crunched when you ate them, providing a little resistance to the tooth that one doesn't normally associate with cooked potatoes. Once again necessity provoked innovation!

But Nature—indefatigable instigator of necessity—was not through for the year. When what I fervently hoped was the final flood of the year hit in October, I learned an entirely different lesson—for which I have no lighthearted label except "go with it." This time the yard was under at least two inches of water, end to end, and the rain that had started Saturday returned on Tuesday for what appeared to be a long stay. By Thursday the flooding was chronic, but I knew there was a big bed of arugula out there (self-sown from last year) and I decided to slosh out and pick some to make an arugula pesto for dinner. I was also lured by the possibility that there might be ripe figs on the riverbank—and the lousy weather might have deterred the birds that usually beat me to them.

So I put on my Gore-Tex shell (inherited from my late husband) and a neighbor's enormous rubber boots—which she concluded long ago that I needed more often than she does—and went out by way of the stone path that skirts my clover circle. The clover path was underwater, but the south pathway, newly planted to ferns and other shady things, didn't seem to have been damaged and wasn't flooded. And there were several fruits floating under my apple tree. I stopped to pick them up and found them perfect, so I put them in my big pockets. When I got to the end of the stone path and stepped out onto the erstwhile clover, I went up to my ankle in mud in a sinkhole just at the edge of the bed, and had trouble getting the giant boot out with my foot in it. But I extricated it, sloshed across the clover path, and carefully picked my way out along the bricks that edge the north side of the path.

It wasn't too hard to walk out—despite the looseness of my boots—since I could step right foot on brick edge, left foot on paver, brick edge to paver, brick edge to paver all the way out. Things were a bloody mess. All the garden trash I had piled in the paths for later cleanup was of course sodden and scattered, and the entire garden looked as desolate as it always does after I am flooded—except this time, at least, the water was clear and the plants and paths were not muddy! The Havahart trap was still open—no skunk had sought shelter from the rain as they often do—and before I began picking arugula, I went up onto the riverbank to see whether there were any new skunk-produced pits. There weren't—she probably didn't want to bother swimming out there.

Things looked okay on the riverbank except for some driftwood scattered on the lawn, and to reward me for my enterprise, several fat ripe figs were hanging right at the front of the tree! I picked the figs—piled them into my right hand—and started back along the south side of the path, abandoning my thoughts of arugula pesto as I realized that there was lots of broccoli that would go to waste unless eaten. Using my free left hand, I snapped off broccoli heads and stuck them stem down in my jacket pockets—over the apples. When the pockets were stuffed (I was surely a bulging sight by now), I gingerly picked my way up the path, trying not to lose figs or broccoli, and made it to the raspberry bed. The soil there was *not* underwater, thank God, and as I had suspected there were ripe raspberries.

So I used my left hand to carefully pluck the ripe raspberries and tuck them gently into the crevices between the figs in my right hand—not an easy task. At one point I dropped a fig and had to pick my way around to the other side of the raspberry bed, not upsetting the handful of figs topped with raspberries to lean over, recover the lost fig, and pick the rest of the raspberries. Back to the stone path, duck around the apple and Asian pear trees, and up the path to the porch. I made it into the house by opening the door latch with my elbow, and got everything upstairs without spilling.

At the sink I emptied my hands and pockets, rinsed the figs, cut them in half into a white bowl, and spread them with the raspberries. Then I cleaned the broccoli, put a pot of water up to boil, microwaved two frozen pesto cubes, added olive oil and grated Parmesan, put pasta into the boiling water for three minutes, added broccoli to the steamer and put it above the boiling pasta for five minutes, tossed the pasta and broccoli with the pesto and Parmesan cheese, added hot pepper flakes, cut up two tomatoes to pile on top, opened a beer, and sat down to eat. What a glorious-looking feast! White pasta with bright green broccoli and red tomatoes and on the side the dish of figs with raspberries. Not bad for a soaking-wet mid-October day!

Hope is the lesson Nature keeps teaching me. She keeps producing. She recovers. She creates beauty out of loss. She forgives us our impatience and frustration and insistence that things turn out the way we planned. They don't. They turn out the way she planned. We need to be willing to sacrifice control to learn adaptation. We need to pay more for food grown by local farmers who can find something to feed us no matter what— even if it's not what we planned on this morning. And that's going to have to be okay. What an important lesson to learn as we face a world that is changing in ways that we don't really want at least partly as fallout from our demand for the things we really thought we needed.

III

Some of the
Other Species

And where does satisfaction come from? I
think it comes from contact with the materials
and lives of this world, from the mutual dependence of creatures upon one another, from
fellow feeling.

—WENDELL BERRY,
The Gift of Good Land, p. 180

CHAPTER TWELVE

How Come?

One of the anxieties that trailed me into widowhood was the assumption that when the house emptied after Alan's death, I would find myself desperately missing the daily interactions that ordinarily fill couples' lives. That no such sense of loss occurred, that I didn't feel bereft of interaction puzzled me and became another mystery to explore. After years of self-examination, I stumbled across a reality that had been staring me in the face all along. As a gardener, I had life all around me. It's just that most of it was not human. As it turned out, the many other species—especially those that appeared invited or uninvited in my garden—were central not only to the maintenance of the planet but to the happiness of my life. My interactions with them, as the following chapters reveal, are often intimate and deep.

Most of us grow up in built environments, paying little attention to the living nonhumans that underpin our survival in ways we seldom notice. As inhabitants of modern industrial societies, we can enjoy the apparently limitless surprises of Nature on TV where they can be made beautiful—and reassuring—even as we ignore how other species in the natural world are actually faring around us. And when one of them forces itself upon us, it is too often a negative (think rats and cockroaches) encounter. Yet as a chronic worrier about the destiny of humanity on the planet, I have long been aware of how completely my own species' future depended on the well-being of *all* those other organisms that flourish below us—or don't—on the biotic pyramid.

It was a book called *Dominion* that markedly shifted my own understanding of how we have come to be where we are. The author is an evolutionary biologist named Niles Eldredge. He points out that before the emergence of *Homo sapiens,* all species survived by depending entirely on the plants and animals in their immediate vicinity, and that all species other than our own still live that way. Depending as they do on a local ecosystem, the members of each population necessarily avoid trashing it since, if they overexploit their surroundings, they will perish from privation or pollution, or both.

Alone among the species, we humans were able to take advantage of a series of physiological changes and such cultural discoveries as fire and agriculture to become capable of living outside our local ecosystems. In the simplest terms this meant that if a group of humans happened to overexploit an ecosystem, they could move on. And they (we) did.

Now, the idea that we were no longer ecosystem people but people who exploit the whole biosphere was not new to me. But what Eldredge said that shifted my vision was the following: *We are the only species that thinks only about our own species.* What a remarkable statement. What does he mean? Here's Eldredge:

> We spend most of our waking (and all of our dreaming) time contemplating details of human life—our own, of course, but also others' lives as we see them impinge on our own . . . There is very little time left over to consider the non-human world . . .
>
> A squirrel spends far more time contemplating members of other species—the trees it feeds on, and takes shelter in, the hawks and cats that might eat it, the birds and rodents that may compete for its food—than any human in this postagricultural world ever does. We think almost exclusively of ourselves and each other . . .

So most "modern" humans (except for agriculturists, biological scientists, and other oddities like me) are almost exclusively interested in one another; and, if the media are any indication, an astonishing proportion of what we like to know about one another has to do with sex or money, or both.

As the world's "first and, so far, *only* inner-directed species," Eldredge says, we seem unable to imagine that we are not entirely self-sufficient, an illusion that seems only to be confirmed by the daily life experiences of a huge proportion of the population. But of course we are not free of "the usual rules of resource limitations that dominate the rest of the living world," and we have gotten away with acting as if we are only because until relatively recently, our numbers were small enough and the size of the planet was large enough that the effect of our self-absorption was not evident. Now our numbers are so much larger that it is.

Since the health of the global system that supports us depends on "the combined health of all the local ecosystems," we *must* pay attention to the other species with which we share our home. Whether we recognize it or not, we still depend on the same natural systems that they do, and if they're in trouble (and many of them surely are) we are too. Isolated as we are from Nature, focused much of the time on electronic illusions, we find this hard to believe.

Consider the arthropods, everything hard-shelled and joint-legged, from insects to barnacles. E. O. Wilson has pointed out that if we should manage to kill the arthropods—and we all sometimes behave as if that's a terrific idea where insects are concerned—we could probably not outlast them by more than a few months.

I must stop here to confess that even as I write this morning I have taken a break from crushing between thumb and forefinger every example, young and old, that I can locate of a gorgeous bug species called the harlequin beetle that has wreaked destruction on my kale and broccoli and brussels sprouts, as well on the generously flowering (and related) cleomes that are usually a feature of my late-summer garden.

I never have insect pests on my crops because, in this riot of vegetation, some natural predator usually takes care of them. So I was entirely unprepared for their onslaught, which meant that I let the infestation proceed much too long before I began my hand-to-bug combat. Ultimately I won, far too late to save the brussels sprouts, almost too late for the kale. And I admit with embarrassment that in this unnatural world we have created, I would have been sorely tempted to exterminate them all—if I could have done so organically. But I digress.

Now that human numbers have multiplied so extravagantly (surely He didn't mean *this* when He said "be fruitful and multiply"), and now that the lavish lifestyles of some of us have expanded so lavishly into ecological space, our destructiveness as a species is frighteningly evident, although apparently not to everyone. There are those who still argue, against reason, that everything is fine and getting better.

But, of course, it is not. We desperately need to look outside ourselves, uncomfortable as it may be to see the world dying around us. "One of the penalties of an ecological education," ecologist Aldo Leopold once wrote,

> is that one lives alone in a world of wounds. Much of the damage inflicted on land is quite invisible to laymen. An ecologist must either harden his shell and make believe that the consequences of science are none of his business, or he must be the doctor who sees the marks of death in a community that believes itself well and does not want to be told otherwise. *Round River*

Which is why I feel comfortable presenting, in a book about death, survival, and the garden, some intimate portraits of my interactions with a few of the other species that share my piece of the planet. Any species would do because they are all part of the fabric of life—the ones featured here are arbitrarily chosen because they are ones I have thought a lot about, willingly or unwillingly as the case may be.

I have harbored chickens in the past, and loved them, but my present yard doesn't seem right for them. Nor do I share my home with the two major species among their plant and animal domesticates to which nonfarming humans normally attend— the Canidae and the Felidae. But I have lived with dogs—ecstatically as a child—and our household has been home to a number of cats over the years, to many of which my children and I were deeply attached, and too many of whom died natural or unnatural deaths.

But I really don't want an animal pet in my ninth decade, and quite by accident I recently confronted part of the reason why. A year or so ago I bought—ostensibly for my grandson's Christmas, but really because I wanted it after seeing it in a farmer friend's living room—a sturdy brown plush footstool so like a real bear cub that when it first took up residence in my living room I used to startle when I walked into the room and caught sight of him/ her. (I am not alone in this reaction—guests startle too.) When Christmas came bringing my son, grandson, and daughter-in-law, who has an actual dog, she gently suggested that I keep the bear here for my grandson's visits, which was her sweetly polite way of telling me she didn't want it in *her* living room. I was secretly happy that she felt that way, and I even got used to the bear and stopped being startled.

And then one day when I caught sight of him unexpectedly, I felt a sudden twinge of guilt because I had been ignoring him. Anyone who can feel guilty about giving insufficient attention to a plush bear whose needs for attention are surely minimal is ill equipped emotionally to live happily with a living pet who will inevitably be full of needs. So I think for my final years, I'll stick with the ones whom we haven't really tamed, the butterflies, the muskrats, and the endangered bees.

CHAPTER THIRTEEN

My Life with Butterflies

In my downstairs office there is a small cabinet, sixteen inches deep, a little over a foot high, and about twenty inches wide. The front of the cabinet has no drawers or doors but is simply a flat surface with a concealed hinge all across the bottom. When you lift up the little brass hooks on either side of the top, the front drops down to reveal an array of six shallow perfectly fitted drawers, each about an inch and a half high, with two little brass drawer pulls. The drawers are only a little bigger than those you might have seen years ago holding spools of thread in a shop that sold sewing supplies, and they are very precisely made, sliding in and out perfectly after more than sixty years. When you pull them open you realize their bottoms are made of composition board soft enough to stick pins in.

Which is what they're for; there are pins sticking in the drawer bottoms on which are impaled moths and butterflies, and a few bees and wasps and beetles—all of them in remarkably good condition after more than sixty years of sticking there that included cross-country shipping from Southern California to New York when I had finally married and settled into a home that could handle my insect collection. I'm quite certain that my folks didn't send the cabinet until I moved to Rockland County, twenty miles north of Manhattan—and in retrospect I'm relieved to know that I never had the chance to display this odd corner of my life to the assorted boyfriends who showed up in my various New York apartments. It was enough that I, a mere woman, could wire lamps and extension cords. I'm afraid a butterfly collection would have done them in.

My butterfly romance began many years before I came to New

York, probably in my father's hometown of Carson, Iowa (pop. fewer than 2,000). Carson had a collection of mounted butterflies and moths—I don't remember where—in the little city hall, I think. And whenever our family returned to Carson to visit my father's oldest brother, my sister and I were always taken to look at the insects. Of course there probably wasn't much else in Carson to interest a five- and seven-year-old. My father grew up in that very small Iowa town, in a household that—as I came to understand—had too many bossy older sisters for his happiness. Which was why he moved to the riverbank when he was twelve.

My father had little to do with most of his family—the eight brothers and sisters of whom he was the youngest. Of the three I knew—two sisters and a brother—only one was still in Carson when Dad married my mother, fathered my sister and me, and took us all back to Iowa so my mother could visit her family in Orange City—several hundred miles to the north.

We always stopped briefly in Carson, visited Dad's oldest brother Uncle Harry and his wife, Aunt Aeolian (a tiny woman who had eight children of her own), looked at the butterflies, and went to the Dye Brothers' Store, which Uncle Harry ran. The store was almost as magical as the butterflies; once we managed to admire off a high shelf, and into our eager hands, a Charlie McCarthy dummy with a movable mouth and a string in the back that you could pull to make Charlie appear to talk.

After one of those trips to Carson, my father made me and my sister butterfly nets from wire coat hangers, old broom handles, and mosquito netting. He also made us a very neat killing bottle, with plaster of paris filling the bottom over a source of some lethal substance—which I seem to remember was chloroform. You swept the butterfly into the net, which you then laid flat on the ground to keep the insect quiet. Then you got hold of the butterfly body through the net, reached gingerly in to get hold of the wings, and, holding it as gently as possible with its two wings folded up over its back, removed it from the net and inserted it into the jar where it was meant to die instantly, without battering its fragile wings.

And here I must take a minute to ensure that there is general understanding of butterfly wings. Underneath all that dazzle, they are colorless chitonous structures that are beautiful only because they are covered with overlapping scales in amazing colors. Some butterflies are quite durable, monarchs for example, their scales adhering tightly—probably to get them through their very long migration south and then back again. And some butterflies are so amazingly fragile that trying to catch and mount one is a fool's game; to touch them even gently is to rub off the colorful scales. Just flapping around on their ordinary lifework does them damage. One solution is to raise them in captivity and let them hatch under more controlled conditions.

My passion for those beautiful fliers was unquestionably stoked very early by a classic girls' book of the early twentieth century called *Girl of the Limberlost*. It was the gloriously romantic story of a young woman—named Elnora Comstock—whose beloved father has drowned tragically and whose impoverished mother treats her miserably even though she is a typically perfect late-Victorian heroine. Although Elnora has no money for adequate school clothes, she is helped by a neighbor and, through her, learns of a collector who will pay money for specimens of the giant moths that hang around the swamplands where Elnora lives.

So she goes out into the swamps, captures, kills, and packages breathtakingly beautiful moths, and in return earns money to get her through high school. I won't tell you how it ends because I don't want to ruin it for you, but things work out okay—and most important, Elnora's adventure set me on a trail that climaxed, in a sense, only a year or so ago, a denouement for which you'll need to wait.

I have no clear recollection of chasing, collecting, and mounting before I was ten or so but I must have been up to something by then because on my tenth birthday, my parents knew they could thrill me with a giant book illustrated only with black-and-white pictures—E. O. Essig's *Insects of Western North America.* This formidable tome is described on its flyleaf as "a manual and textbook for students in colleges and universities, and a handbook for county, state, and federal entomologists and agriculturists, as well as foresters, farmers, gardeners, travelers and lovers of nature." And, of course, ten-year-olds. This thousand-page challenge meant so much to me that when I took a high school course in leathercraft, I made Essig a handsome cover made of Moroccan leather, lined with thin suede, and embossed with my initials in alligator. I confess that I still have both the book and its cover—and I even consult it occasionally though I am no longer in western North America.

In another much less daunting book, I earned exactly how to raise butterflies and moths. Directed by that, I raised some gorgeous fliers to adulthood. On the wild anise that grew in Southern California vacant lots (there *were* vacant lots in Southern California then!), I sometimes found the green sweet-smelling larvae of anise swallowtails on my way home from school. This marvelously ingenious insect could, when disturbed, turn itself into a faux snake by curling its head down, thereby swelling the round spot on its thorax into something that looked like an eye, and then send out a forked yellow scent organ that looked like a tongue. I loved the odor of that caterpillar, and raised several of them to maturity. When one of them lashed her hindquarters to a heavy anise stalk with her own silk, then stretched down and out to transform herself into a chrysalis, I spent hours watching, waiting for the caterpillar to shed her skin and transform herself from gaudy insect to pale green and nearly invisible chrysalis, swinging in the wind, waiting to mature.

The two most memorable butterfly-farming adventures of my youth involved some tiny eggs I found on a leaf, and a gulf fritillary that I raised to adulthood from a captured caterpillar. I don't remember where I found the eggs—although I know we were living at the time in Hollywood. And I remember being thrilled at the prospect of actually raising a butterfly from eggs as opposed to captured larvae.

So I took a metal can, put some dirt in the bottom, and every afternoon when I came home from school I checked to see whether the eggs had hatched. Finally, they did, and tiny, tiny larvae came out. I can't remember how I knew what to give them to eat, but whatever it was—and I know now it wouldn't have mattered much—I raised them successfully through several molts until they were perhaps half an inch long. They weren't very endearing—smooth, gray, and laterally striped, with a tendency to curl into a ball, and none of the glamour of the caterpillars I was used to, the bright green striped and spotted tomato sphinx with a horn for a tail, or the subtly beige-and-pink grape sphinx—but they were my young ones and I loved them.

And then one day I urged my mother to come look at my success and she looked, drew back, and exclaimed in horror, "Those are cutworms." And, alas, dear reader, they were. Ugly, nasty cutworms, which Mom insisted I destroy immediately. It was quite a disappointment, although as a serious gardener who has lost many young seedlings to cutworms, I now fully understand her horror.

My other adventure was less disappointing, and much more thought provoking. As I noted earlier, it's very difficult to get certain very fragile butterflies and moths into a collection in any sort of condition. Their wings tend to get battered even before you go after them with a net—and the process of capture doesn't help. The gulf fritillary—a gorgeously fragile insect with pinkish orange coloring on its underside decorated with shining silver spots—was one of them.

So when I found a gulf fritillary caterpillar on a neighbor's passion vine, I realized I could raise her myself and have a perfect specimen. I broke off a piece of the vine whose leaves she was chewing, took her home, and put her in a lidded jar with holes punched in the top. And every day I hiked up the street to the neighbor's vine and stole a few fresh leaves for my captive to eat. My effort was successful. She grew and grew and ultimately hung herself up by her hind legs and turned into a chrysalis.

And then the wait began. You could see through the semi-transparent walls of the chrysalis as the caterpillar began the process of turning herself into a butterfly—as maturity approached, you could even begin to see the color of the wings. It was very exciting, in a slow nineteenth-century sort of way, and worth every minute once the butterfly began to hatch. The chrysalis broke open, along the back midline as I remember, and the wet adult, wings crumpled against her body, pushed herself out and hung damply from the now empty chrysalis by her six long legs. And then, clinging tightly, she began to pump her slender body, forcing fluid into the channels of her wings, which gradually expanded into a breathtaking glory of rose and gold and silver. She was a perfect specimen. But of course, I couldn't kill her. How could anyone watch that amazing transformation and then dunk the result into a killing jar? I let her go and never did get to mount a perfect gulf fritillary.

My parents were unfailingly sympathetic to their daughter's passion. Once when they drove back to Iowa on a trip that did not include my sister and me, my father captured in his hat on the main street of Pella, Iowa, and brought home to his excited girls, one of the giant silk moths that were essentially aliens in sunny California. It was a cecropia moth with a five-inch wingspread, a treasure I still have in my insect collection. And although my mother was seriously taken aback when she heard her innocent daughter calling loudly to the teenage boy next door, "David, come over, the swallowtails are mating!" neither she or my father ever discouraged my interest in all phases of the insects' lives.

Consider the insect cabinet in my office, which my father made and gave me for Christmas the same year he gave my sister a handmade cedar chest suited to her more immediate hopes for marriage. My father was decidedly *not* a fine cabinetmaker by instinct or temperament. He was an engineer who could build and fix almost anything, but beauty was not his forte; strength was. When my mother asked him to make something, she risked getting something pretty crude, but if my father built it, we women all agreed that an elephant could stand on it.

Across the street from our house, however, lived a childless couple, the Willises, who were everything we were not—odd, English, bookish, and meticulous. It was Mr. Willis—who had employment doing research for movie studios—who handed down to my father, who subsequently left it to me, my stupendous corduroy-bound 1912 *Heritage Dictionary*.

I don't know what, if anything, Mr. Willis constructed for his own household—I recall no handsome pieces of hand-built furniture in his home—but he knew someone with a cabinetmaking shop. And when my father came up with the idea of making my sister Barbara and myself something special for Christmas, that's where Mr. Willis took him. And, painstakingly I am sure, Dad learned enough about the art of fine cabinetmaking to construct something for me that has lasted well beyond his lifetime. It's carefully joined and finished to an extent remarkable for my father, and I'll bet an elephant could stand on it.

And so I grew up. My plans to become an entomologist—given an extra boost in adolescence by discovering how few women were in the field—were discouraged by the discovery that the actual profession would involve not raising and mounting butterflies but mind-numbing tasks such as counting the hairs on the back end of a tachinid fly. I wasn't interested in that. Indeed, I'm only even familiar with Tachinidae because they so often thwarted my caterpillar-raising efforts.

I frequently found little white projections growing on the backs of my captive caterpillars, and those larvae collapsed and died before they matured. Trying to figure out what was going on, I came across—in the everlastingly valuable Essig of course—

the family Tachinidae: ". . . a large economic family of beneficial flies, the larvae of which are parasitic on innumerable destructive pests. The good done in this way cannot be estimated as it is so obscure and ramifying and we can only say that these flies play a considerable part as a natural check to plant-feeding insects." I'll say. However many giant green sphinx caterpillars I found on my tomato plants, I never managed to raise one to maturity since some tachinids always beat me to it, laid eggs, and used the caterpillar's body as dinner for its young. Those white spines were the cocoons the larvae made after they had finished hollowing out my livestock.

So the possibility that I might be reduced in adulthood to studying tachinid flies discouraged me from entomology, and a few absorbing books like Paul de Kruif's *Men Against Death* led me elsewhere. Here in breathless prose were stories of heroic doctors such as Ignaz Semmelweis who saved women from death from puerperal fever by teaching doctors to wash up before they touched laboring women. Ignoring the subtext, that his discovery was disparaged as too simple and thus humiliating to the majesty of the other physicians, and that Semmelweis died in a mental hospital, I decided to be a doctor.

I got through pre-med, although by my senior year, I switched to a zoology/chemistry major, which freed me from German and physics—and from the seemingly endless labs in which one dissected formaldehyde-soaked animals. And when I graduated and came to New York looking for a job in journalism, one of the things I most wanted to see—after the stores on Fifth Avenue whose names were familiar to me from my mother's copies of *Vogue* magazine—was a display I had seen pictured in a copy of *Natural History*. It was a great vertical piece of tree on which thousands of monarch butterflies were mounted, clinging in curtains as they did in their winter quarters in Latin America. When I went to the Museum of Natural History for the first time, that was what I looked for. I was still flitting.

So I married, gave birth twice, and when my sons were young, I made them butterfly nets out of wire coat hangers and broom handles and went chasing butterflies with them. And when once we went to the Yucatán—a vacation paid for by my in-laws, who had offered us the Caribbean—the children caught beautiful tropical butterflies, which we learned to kill by pinching their thoraces (butterfly throats). We brought them home with us to relax and mount—and they too are in my insect case, a reminder of how readily we all traveled and took before the era of "take only footprints, leave only pictures."

And once when the children were perhaps eight and ten, we drove out to Brooklyn to the Butterfly Art Jewelry Company, which sold mounted butterflies and moths, cocoons, mounting pins, mounting boards, and the like. There we bought a live cocoon of the one insect I had yearned to see since I had learned of it in *Girl of the Limberlost*, a giant pale green ghost called a luna moth, with long tails flaring out from its back wings. We brought the cocoon home with us and laid it in a box with some small oak tree branches, which we kept on a table in the second-floor hall so we wouldn't miss any signs of hatching.

The box sat on the hall table for months, until one day when I noticed that the end of the cocoon was wet, dampened by the saliva that the emerging moth was producing to soften its papery shroud. I shouted excitedly to the children, who came running. Gradually the papery cover gave way to a small hole and we all watched, impatiently, as first one long downy pale green leg and then a second one emerged from the opening. The young moth kept working away at the hole, pushing and widening for what seemed like hours.

I began to worry that being indoors where the air was dried by our forced-air heating system—instead of outdoors where the rain and snow would keep it softened—had so toughened the cocoon that the moth couldn't get out. So I decided to help it a little. With manicure scissors, I made a careful little slit along one side of the hole. Still the moth struggled, seeming to make little progress in dragging its giant body out of the cocoon. So I cut a bit more, making its exit easier. And finally, out it plopped, a fat pale green body with its potentially giant pale green wings damply crumpled around it as the creature struggled to climb up a branch where it could hang and pump fluid into its wings to expand them fully before they hardened.

But the wretched thing could not hang on. The damp moth kept crawling up the rough branch, waving its long slender front legs and tentatively grabbing on—and then falling off, its legs too weak to hold up the weight of its own heavy body. My efforts to help Nature along had been hideously misguided. I had destroyed—in trying to help—something I had yearned to see for years. The moth huddled on the bottom of the box, its half-crumpled wings hardening as we watched. It would never fly. It was for me a formidable and unforgettable lesson. Sometimes struggle is part of the plan.

After months in a cocoon, the luna had to use its legs to work its way into the world to get them ready for their next task—to cling to a branch, wings down, pumping fluid from that heavy body into the crumpled wings to elate them to their full glory. And I had ruined everything. The children took it much better than I did. I suspect my pain displaced theirs. After all, they had not grown up on *Girl of the Limberlost*.

It would have been sad if my loving relationship with insects had ended there—if I had gone on to see them only as enemies in the garden. But my romance wasn't over. My failures, like my more frequent successes, were obviously mere prelude to our family's most triumphant moth experiences. Several years after the luna moth tragedy, my older son Adam flung himself off the bus from a summer enrichment class—he was about twelve years old I think—wildly excited and brandishing one of those little round metal containers that used to hold typewriter ribbons. One of the children in his class had brought to school a battered but living giant silk moth. With the help of their teacher, Mr. Bartolo, the class had identified it as a polyphemus, a creature named—because of the large eye-spots on its hindwings—after the one-eyed giant of Greek mythology. Since the moth was in bad shape after its capture, the teacher dispatched it—with alcohol, I think. But, struggling to live out its life mission, it laid several dozen tiny eggs as it died.

Adam knew my cutworm story, and he wanted those eggs— guaranteed by their provenance not to hatch cutworms. Fortunately, he had little competition. I suspect that our child neighbors—so out of touch with Nature that they never stole fruit because they didn't recognize it on my neighbor's trees— had no sense of moth-egg potential, and even less interest in what the eggs might produce.

Adam took off the lid of his little round can and showed me the eggs, after which we hunted up a butterfly book to see what polyphemus caterpillars ate. Birch leaves were their preferred food, and Adam knew where in the neighborhood he could find some. So we set up an old aquarium, put in some birch twigs, and laid the eggs on top. Then every day we changed the leaves to keep them fresh until the babies hatched. We didn't have to wait long. Within ten days tiny prickly green crawlers—thread-like beings with large hungry heads they needed food to grow into—swarmed over the leaves looking for an edge to chew.

Once they had fastened themselves on, we got a giant pickle jar, put a smaller water-filled jar in the bottom, and put birch branches into that. On this fresh foliage, the little chewers, eating ravenously and steadily, grew and grew, going through several molts as their bodies began to outgrow their heads.

Until summer school was over, Adam raced home after class every day anxious to see what had happened to his trophies. Caterpillars grow by molting; when their skin gets too tight, they cling to a branch, the skin splits along the back, and the growing crawler wiggles out. Since they didn't grow at exactly the same rate, there was often something to watch. They grew rapidly. By fall they would be two inches long.

As the summer progressed, and the caterpillars grew larger and fatter, we began waiting eagerly for the climax—the start of spinning. Polyphemus caterpillars make large parchment-like cocoons composed of dried leaves and the tough silk they spin, binding the cocoon to a branch for the winter. Inside that cocoon, the crawler begins the transformation from worm to flier, turning first into a smooth brown pupa case, with—sticking out the side—a little pump-handle cover for the future moth's long tongue. And over time inside the pupa case, the transformation into flier that proceeds more visibly in free-hanging chrysalids progressed in the dark.

And one day, one of the caterpillars—we must have had ten or twelve full-sized ones by now—began to spin, pulling a leaf around her. Then another began, and another. At last all the caterpillars—none of them infested by parasitic flies—had encased themselves for the winter. By this time our little experiment was enclosed in a cage of four window screens, nailed together on the sides, with the branches sitting in jars in the middle. When the young ones had all tucked themselves in, we put a screen over the top and left them to go through the winter on their own.

It's hard when you're twelve to keep your mind on a passive extended project over the long term. But Adam, usually quick to use up novelty, never lost interest in the progress of the eggs he had hatched. And so as winter turned into spring, we all began to watch for the moths to emerge. None of us had ever seen this happen—successfully! The aborted luna moth hatching was our only experience with a giant moth—and it was not a good one. So I'm not sure any of us really believed that we were going to get a polyphemus, much less a cageful of them.

But one day, working in the yard, I glanced over at the cage and there it was. A huge, gorgeous moth, hanging from one of the window screens, very slowly fanning its wings to dry. This time it was I who met Adam with a yell of excitement when he came home from class. "One hatched," I yelled as he got off the bus.

I have no clear recollection of what transpired over the next few weeks as the remaining cocoons released their beautiful fliers. I'm sure we let some of them go—to reproduce on nearby trees. I know we killed and mounted several of them; I have two in my case downstairs. Together with his artist dad who drew the parts Nature couldn't provide—the original moth struggling to lay her eggs, and a very accurate picture of a grown caterpillar (not available to stuff for mounting)—Adam put together a framed display of the life cycle of the polyphemus moth with which he won a blue ribbon in the 4-H exhibits at the Rockland County fair. He was smilingly proud of the whole enterprise, and I was rewarded beyond all my expectations by finally having participated in the life cycle of such a beautiful creature.

I had another momentary high in my long-term relationship with butterflies when Alan and I moved to Piermont. We planted the garden and the riverbank while we were still gutting the house and living in Congers. And we used to take breaks from our labors by sitting out on the boardwalk congratulating ourselves for our wisdom in having chosen this place. One day in October as we were sitting talking I noticed a monarch flying down the river. I wrote in my journal that day:

> As we sit on the boardwalk talking Alan and I are both continually distracted by Monarch butterflies passing by. When the third one passes within 3 minutes, I realize that I have always heard about Monarchs flying down the Hudson. My God, we're on the Monarch flyway! Before we go in we see at least 10.

So *my* God, or someone's, had rearranged my life so I could watch the monarchs migrate to one of those places where they hung in curtains through the winter.

Several years later, I came home from a walk to find a message on my answering machine. It was my son Adam, breathless with excitement, reporting from his woodland home in Mississippi: "Mom, you're not going to believe this. I had a luna moth sitting on my hand." And the next day, he e-mailed me pictures of a gorgeous luna moth, clinging in one photo to the wall of his house, and, in another, hanging in a nearby tree. And I wrote him to say that the pictures almost made me cry. And they did.

So when I went to Mississippi the next spring to welcome my first grandson into the world, I saw a video of this wild thing that was even more remarkable than the still photos. Which is the moment, I think, to introduce the moral of this long story, that touching the natural world, keeping some contact with Nature time, is not a romantic antiquarian notion. Sometime before the luna moth, and before my son Adam had moved to Mississippi to teach, he told me a story about the meaning to him of the moth-raising event that touched me deeply. We were discussing a recent *New Yorker* article by a critic and father who was writing of his ambiguity and near despair about the media world his sons lived in. My son is a professor now, and is also a writer and musician, deeply rooted in the natural world despite a performance life that is often necessarily nocturnal and rootless. "I almost wrote him a letter," he said, "to ask him why he didn't take his kids out on a hike or have a catch with them. I was going to talk about my polyphemus moths."

And as I watch my grandson grow, I am assured that another generation of my family will grow up learning to love moths— and their butterfly relatives too—and through them learning to love and respect the pace of the natural world. As for me, I'm planning a lot of visits to Mississippi, at least one during that part of the year when the lunas are most likely to be flying. I swear I'm going to see a living one—in the flesh, so to speak—before I die.

CHAPTER FOURTEEN

Why Not Try Rice?

By the time I finally got around to it, I'd tolerated years of teasing about how dumb I was not to just grow rice. My friends weren't pushing me to add grains to the foods I produce; they simply thought I should welcome to my garden at least one species likely to be enthusiastic about the conditions I offered. Given the fact that I crop on land that floods—and floods a lot—most of my friends couldn't avoid noticing that much of what I grow does not flourish in boggy soil. I do have a bed of "no-bog" cranberries from which I harvest a couple of quarts each year, but I planted them with no intention of testing their desire to become bog cranberries. They seem to *survive* the floodings, as do most of my fruits and vegetables, sometimes sullenly, but they have given no indication that they are truly gratified to be underwater part of the time.

But multiple floods on successive days late one winter finally convinced me that global warming was telling me something. I needed a reason not to mourn when the garden went underwater; it was time to try something that grows happily in flooded fields—rice. I had a spare plot in which to try it, having learned over time that I could grow much more than I could eat year-round, so I set out to find rice seeds.

They were harder to locate than I had imagined they would be, but ultimately I found them in a catalog from Bountiful Gardens in California. And, with some difficulty—the Web site didn't work for me, an all-too-frequent condition when you are too old for an iPod—I got the packet of seeds. The instructions said to plant the seeds indoors and transplant them out into "mucky" soil when they had spouted "true leaves."

I carefully spaced out one hundred seeds in a large, oval pot, watered them in, covered the pot with plastic wrap, and assumed nothing would happen. I tend to be suspicious of things I have never grown, and take for granted that my first, second, and sometimes third attempts will fail. But my skepticism was, at least initially, unwarranted. In no time at all up came one hundred little spear-like shoots, which were soon followed out of the planting mix by a grassy leaf. Was this a "true leaf"? Who knew. I had never grown rice before. I took off the plastic wrap and when the seedlings got very leggy and tall, I cut off the tops as I used to do with onion seedlings, to make them grow thicker. In retrospect, I'm pretty sure that wasn't a good idea.

Still, the plants kept growing, and that's when it struck me that I was going to have to plant out one hundred of these skinny little tots, a task similar in its physical demand to planting out onion seedlings. I don't grow onions from seeds anymore, but from small onions called "sets"—at least partly because of the problem of setting out the plantlets, many of which have been lost indoors from what is called "damping off" before they ever have a chance to go outside. The survivors must be taken up in clumps, carefully separated out, and individually set several inches apart in holes punched in the intended bed, each held by its slender neck and carefully watered in so it settles not too deeply, and so on, and on. Sets are just little onions you push up to their necks into well-dug ground. The rice seemed to promise a similar challenge.

Moreover, I am not as young as I used to be. Some time ago I was forced to recognize the fact that I could no longer crouch. It was the sharp pain in my right knee that suddenly assaulted me as I walked downstairs several years ago that precipitated that knowledge. It seemed mysterious to me that something should have gone wrong just like that, with no warning. So I did a bit of doctoring, got as far as learning that there was nothing visible on an X-ray, and decided to see what time would do. Time actually did the trick. Still, during the time when I was hobbling around I was stunned to find one day, going back through my journal, an entry that started, "I think I wrecked both my knees today . . ." I suppose that counts as a warning.

Knees aside, I had to get the rice planted out and thought I knew something about how to do it from old movies. The idea of planting rice seedlings evoked memories of Italian actress Silvana Mangano, deliciously sweaty in the fields of Italy in the 1949 film *Bitter Rice*. I also seemed to recall German actress Luise Rainer in *The Good Earth,* a hit back in the 1930s, playing a suffering Chinese peasant standing knee-deep in water, inserting one rice plant after another into a field of muck. I imagined it would amuse others as I was amused to picture me as a peasant, just like Luise, as I set out my rice plants. Unfortunately, when I smilingly mentioned this fantasy to a couple of my friends, no one had the faintest idea what I was talking about. Is everyone else too young or did those images make a particular impression on me? I felt sure I had known about the demands of rice planting from infancy.

The job wasn't easy, but someone had given me a kneeling stool that made it possible. So in early May I took a rusty, cement-covered concrete pointing tool inherited from my father and made trenches down the bed. Then I crouched on the stool and laid in the rice plants roots-down, about two inches apart, watered them in with transplant solution, and pushed dirt over their exposed roots and up to their necks. It took just over an hour to plant them all, and although they looked feeble, it's always hard to predict from the early returns what will do well. My chard looks truly terminal when I plant it out and it grows up to my armpits. The rice sprouts seemed okay the next morning, although an unbelievably heavy downpour had pelted them with water all night. They liked water, I assumed; they probably had a grand time.

Over the next few weeks, I watched and waited, and waited . . .

and waited for the seedlings to send out their next leaves. They never did. They didn't die; they just failed to grow. Whatever the rice wanted, in order to live out its destiny, I had utterly failed to provide it. I suspect that my early pruning had cut off their first "true leaves." Meanwhile, I had an essentially empty bed with a lot of eagerly growing weeds and what looked like a few straggling grass spears in it. Its appearance dismayed me and seemed to call for a lot of explanation and apology to those visitors who came to admire the crops of a successful mini farmer!

Finally, in late June, I gave up. I went carefully over the bed, found ten rice youngsters (of the hundred planted) that seemed to have at least a trace of life in them, and replanted them in two rows running across the front of the bed. It was touch-and-go for a while, but eventually they took hold and began to grow another leaf or two. And then, in July, the rabbit came. I journaled that morning with a yelp of outrage.

> I was doing a morning walk through the garden and discovered that the rice plants—the ten pitiful rice plants that I managed to recover from the totally unsuccessful planting of 100—were being eaten, apparently by a rabbit.

I guessed immediately that it was not a woodchuck since there was untouched broccoli nearby and woodchuck MO is to take out the broccoli first—and definitively. When I could recover myself enough to think, I understood that the truly profound question this garden raid provoked was, "How does a Hudson River Valley rabbit develop a taste for rice plants?" Rice is *never* grown here.

"Oh, rabbits eat anything," you might respond. But they don't. I have to protect only certain plants in the spring garden—young lettuce and peas and beans are some of them. Granted, there are a few plants that are so attractive to rabbits, you can't keep them out even by fencing. I tried once to grow red clover as a cover crop, thinking I had the bed protected. Yet despite all my fencing efforts, the tiny plants were nibbled down so repeatedly and completely that the clover and I gave up. My rice-eating bunny, though, defied logic. She was astonishingly selective—eating only rice, not the wheatgrass growing next to it or the carrots in the bed right across the path, no more than a hop away.

But the plants didn't die. In August I wrote to some friends in California that the plants—all ten of them—were starting to produce beautiful little pendulous grain stalks. I wondered briefly whether the rabbit would start in on the grain too. She didn't, but the whole project had been a lot of trouble just to get forty-odd grains of rice that I didn't even bother to harvest.

And I'm still puzzled by that rabbit's taste buds. Why rice and not the next-door carrot tops? Bugs Bunny would have eaten the whole bed. And Peter Rabbit risked being crushed by Mr. McGregor's spade just to get at carrots. You'll be interested to know what I learned from the Web about this: There were 423,000 hits for rabbits and carrots; pet-rabbit diet sites don't recommend carrots tops for every day; but best of all there's a very popular musical group in Mexico called Rabbits and Carrots. None of which explains my nibbled rice.

CHAPTER FIFTEEN

Muskrats, Dahlias, and an Italian

I was relieved to see the bulging plastic bag behind my gate when I came home from shopping. My neighbor had remembered that I wanted the cleanings from her cats' litter box to pour into the massive hole I had found the day before and diagnosed as a muskrat den. My diagnosis of what might have produced the hole was not casual. I had seen in my yard—and ultimately caught—two muskrats earlier in the summer. And while finding a big hole next to a mound of dirt would normally lead me to jump to a woodchuck conclusion, I was almost certain I didn't have a woodchuck this time.

The animal I had glimpsed several times before I set out to trap it was sitting upright on the riverbank or eating clover on my path, very near an untouched bed of broccoli. And as I mentioned before, when you have a woodchuck, the broccoli goes first. No wonder those beasts get so big and healthy: They love the whole brassica family we nutritionists are always urging everyone to eat—broccoli, brussels sprouts, kale, but especially broccoli. Since there was no broccoli damage, I was convinced I had no woodchuck.

As for muskrats, I think I have spotted them in the water, and I have occasionally found holes on the north side of my riverbank that appear to lead to the river, but this is the first year I was aware of *having* a muskrat. Until now muskrats have never done damage in my garden, and since they are rather cute, I have never waged war on them as I do whenever I think a woodchuck has found its way to my small plot of land. But this year was different.

Last year I had decided that my rather haphazard approach to the flower beds on the riverbank was not producing the effect I intended, and since I was the happy recipient of a two-hundred-dollar gift certificate at a fancy nursery, I spent it all on gorgeous perennials, among them, both tall and shorter versions of one of my favorite flowers—platycodon, popularly known as balloon flowers—whose buoyant-looking five-sided balloon-shaped buds open to big violet-blue stars. To plant in front of them, I bought three feathery-leaved coreopsis plants, one covered with tiny daisy-like flowers in pale orange, the others covered with the same sort of flowers in pale yellow. I thought the combination was stunning.

They were doing well and were in full bloom when the muskrat struck. Now that I have gone on the Web and studied muskrats, I am aware that they live preferentially on aquatic vegetation. They will apparently eat almost anything that grows in water, but they can also survive on dry-land crops—corn, soybeans, grains, and sugarcane as well as various grasses—and clover. And, as I learned unhappily, balloon flowers. I assume it is the lack of aquatic vegetation in my particular section of the Hudson River that explains why this muskrat decided to chew to the ground all my flowers, including the asters that were growing vigorously and would have bloomed in the fall.

The raid convinced me I needed to do something about what I had until then assumed was a cute and harmless animal. I must introduce here the fact that I had, painting the trim on my house at the time, a handsome graying Italian man with a flirtatious manner who had pointed out to me several times that I had an animal. "I know, Joe," I said, disgustedly, "and he's eaten all my flowers." He smiled beguilingly, cocked his finger and thumb like he had a gun, and bragged that he would get him for me. "Bang, bang." He did that several times when he glimpsed the animal in the course of his work around the house. I urged him to "blast away," but it became clear that his aggressiveness toward my intruder was no more than what he imagined to be charming talk.

So I got out my Havahart trap, since my usual approach to unwanted visitors is not lethal. And realizing that I had no idea what it would take to attract this creature, I put in a piece of apple, a piece of carrot, and a section of melon—no effort too extreme, I felt—and set the trap very divertingly among the leaves of a plant on the riverbank. And the next day I had caught her. (As you will learn shortly, my sex-assignment here is *not* an effort to be politically correct.)

One of the problematic things about a Havahart trap is that if you actually intend to have-a-heart you have to take whatever you've caught in it and release it someplace where it has the possibility of surviving. This has been a difficult problem with skunks, whom I seem to catch without intending to, but it is a problem I have taken on and mastered since I found a large unmonitored patch of woods and realized that skunks didn't/couldn't spray when a trap was too confining, and disdained spraying as they walked away after release. But since my current visitor was semi-aquatic, not someone I could release in the woods with any hope she would survive, I needed to take her to a riverbank—ideally one very far from mine.

As it happened, I discovered my trapping success too late in the day to take the animal anywhere that night, and in the morning a perfect solution occurred to me. My painter lived near the river several miles north of me, and he had a truck. It would be easy for him to take the trap and release her for me—especially as he had repeatedly made his gallant offer to "take care of it." So I walked out front to where Joe was getting ready to paint and told him I had caught the muskrat, and that since I had to be away most of the day, I wanted him to take her with him when he left and release her at the waterfront in his own community. He looked at me, adorably feigning shock, but he reluctantly agreed to do the deed. I pointed out the trap sitting by my back gate, and left for my appointment. When I came home late that afternoon he had already left—and the trap was also gone. Next morning

I asked him where the trap was and he looked at me soulfully—a look he was good at. "It's in my truck," he said. And then he confessed: "I was going to lie to you about what happened so I put the trap in my trunk and was going to tell you I had let the animal go down by the river."

"So what *did* happen?" I asked warily.

"Well," he said, "when I came out here to get the trap she had had babies."

The best I could muster was, "You're kidding!" Joe went on to explain that by the time he stopped painting and went back to look at the trap, the babies had been born and were squirming around and getting caught in the trap's wire-mesh floor. He was so upset by this childbirth disaster that he decided to help by turning the trap upside down so the mother could lie on the solid metal top of the trap; then he could drop the babies through the mesh onto her waiting belly to nurse. It was a romantic Madonna-and-child vision, perhaps not surprising in an Italian painter who listened all day to classical music as he worked. But it was a vision that took absolutely no account of Nature's realities.

So he turned the trap over, the trapdoors fell open, and Mom took off, leaving her newborns in Joe's hands. She was considerably less worried about them than Joe was. "Where did she go?" I asked, as politely as possible.

"She took off toward the river," he said.

I'm afraid I swore. Joe had taken the babies, he assured me, and laid them tenderly among the plants along the edges of my garden. They couldn't possibly survive, of course, but I was furious. I had caught the animal that was demolishing my flowers and he had released her to continue her work. I was not nice about it.

The motherhood aspect of it cut no ice with me. Even before I learned from Wikipedia that muskrats could have two to three litters a year of six to eight young each, I wasn't worried about their future, but my own as a gardener. Joe tried to calm me down by saying he would reset the trap. "You're kidding," I said for the second time that day. "Don't you know anything about wildlife? Do you imagine any animal is going to go right back into the same trap she's just been traumatized in?"

"Why not?" he asked. I doubt that my response was educational. Joe reset the trap and I gave him some apple to put in it, but of course, she was not recaptured and Joe and I changed the subject over the next few days as he finished my outdoor painting and left with the thought that he might be back in colder weather to paint inside. He *was* a good painter.

Meanwhile I had no more flowers for muskrats to eat, but I did notice holes in some of the beds, and it looked as if someone was digging in the carrot bed and gnawing at the roots. Some of the dill was also being eaten, and although a rabbit had been making occasional sorties all summer, dill was never its target. So in one of the beds where I thought I saw signs of someone visiting, I reset the trap, this time with a broken-open melon that I assumed would be irresistible.

It was late October when I set the trap, and no one took the bait. And fall being what it is in the garden, I just left the trap there as the melon dried up and frost hit the remaining peppers and eggplant—much more belatedly than in pre-climate-change times. Since I plant garlic on the waning of the first full moon after the first frost—which fell that year a week or so before Thanksgiving—I was spending time in the late garden, and since I had taken to burying my kitchen garbage directly in empty spots in the vegetable beds was often out there even when there was nothing to pick.

So one day right after Thanksgiving, as I was wondering if I should try again to rebait the trap for whatever had been grubbing around the carrots, I looked over and noticed that both sides of the trap were down—there was my muskrat! As it happened my Italian painter was back, working inside. And my first thought was "Aha. Joe can take the muskrat to the river."

So I went indoors, waved my arms to get him to take the earphones off so he could hear me, and teasingly said, "Well, Joe, life gives very few people the opportunity to completely redeem themselves. But Nature has just given you another chance. I caught the muskrat in an unbaited trap. And since she's already had her kids, you can take her along tonight." This time it was he who said, "You're kidding." But I wasn't, and he took the full trap and brought it back the empty the next morning. I was through with the muskrat.

But the muskrat was not through with me. On the twenty-eighth of December, a week after it had been twelve degrees when I woke up, it was sixty outside, so I went out to walk the yard, trying to avoid noticing that there was lots of cleanup to do out there. That was when I realized I should really take up my dahlia tuber for the winter—assuming that it was not already too late. I had only one dahlia, and for something that had begun as a plant I did not even want, it had outdone itself on my behalf.

I had even a single dahlia only because one late-spring day as I was walking in from my driveway, which is next to the community garden, one of the gardeners whom I don't know well asked me if I would like a dahlia tuber; she had some left from a package she had bought. I hesitated. I don't grow many flowers except on the riverbank, and when I do grow them, I tend to favor perennials. So I asked, "Those are the ones you have to dig and store over the winter, right?" And she said "Yes," and I said, as kindly as possible, "Thanks, Sema, but I don't think so. I don't want to fuss with them over the winter."

So I went in the gate, put away the groceries, and went back out to work in the garden . . . feeling guilty. This, of course, is something I'm very good at since I was raised by a loving mother who, instead of getting angry with me when I did something she judged wrong, cried at me instead. There's nothing like getting cried at to produce a person readily given to guilt. So I walked back out my gate, called over to Sema in the community garden, and told her I thought I *would* like a dahlia. She brought me a star-shaped clutch of tubers maybe two inches across, and because the beds were all spoken for by that time, I put it in a bed where it was surrounded by potatoes.

After that I ignored it, until one day I realized that as the potato foliage was dying down, the dahlia foliage was coming up. I had the bed covered with a Quonset hut made of hog-wire fencing that I use over beds containing plants that might otherwise sprawl. Plants like eggplant, peppers, and broccoli grow up through the four-by-four openings and don't fall over when they get heavy-topped. And as the dahlia grew, I could see that it was going to need all the support it could get. It topped out at about seven feet and began bearing deep pink supper-plate-sized flowers—in bunches. It was stunning, and when heavy winds off the river came rushing up my wind tunnel of a yard and some of the very brittle stalks broke over, the broken-over dahlia went right on blooming, lying on the brick path on the side away from the wind, and turning its flowering heads up to the light.

As this performance was going on, I realized that on the riverside corner of the bed and abutting my stone wall, there had appeared under the potato foliage a depressed area that seemed to be someone's runway, heading right under the wall. One of the problems with my Quonset hut support system is that once plants are growing up through these cages, the cages themselves—about six feet long—are not movable until fall when things die down. So even though the potatoes had died back and made this runway visible, the dahlia was still thrusting strongly through multiple holes in the support and was impossible to extract without completely destroying it. I managed to reach through and stuff some large rocks into the depressed area and decided I would let it go until frost killed the dahlia. It was after this discovery that I caught the second muskrat in the empty trap, so I felt comfortable that the problem was solved.

Which brings me to the early-winter day I went out to take

up the dahlia tuber. I pulled off the now dead remains of the huge stalks that had grown up through the supporting cage. This allowed me to remove the cage entirely, which was when I noticed that in the corner where I had formerly noticed a path, there was now an enormous mound of earth. When I went in and tried to find the source of all that dirt, it became clear that the hole it concealed ran under the wall and up into the planter bed behind it, so I began to dismantle the wall, taking off a huge slab of sandstone that partially covered the top. Sure enough, there was a large den underneath.

I was stopped cold, and, realizing this problem was not going to be easily solved, I went back to take up the dahlia bulb. I plunged my spade into the soil about three inches out from the center of the plant and discovered that I had cut through three tubers.

Clearly I needed to start farther out from the stem. So I did, and I unearthed the most enormous cluster of dahlia tubers—at least a foot across. The plant I had once turned down had grown stunningly productive, produced bouquets of gorgeous flowers, and then set a tuber so immense I had no idea how to store it. I brought it inside, called the person who had given it to me, and asked what I was supposed to do with this giant. Sema had no idea. She had never saved one.

But the distraction of the dahlia had allowed my mind to go to work on the muskrat problem. After several desperate struggles with woodchucks, I had learned that if you put used kitty litter down any burrow they dig, they leave—deeply offended, I assume. So I called a next-door neighbor who has cats and said I wanted something much less attractive than her last gift of Christmas cookies. I wanted used kitty litter. I had no guarantee, of course, that muskrats would be as vulnerable to—and as appalled by— the scent of cat leavings, as woodchucks clearly are, but I thought there was no harm trying to make the space uninhabitable, even though I hoped that it no longer had an occupant.

But I didn't immediately use the kitty litter that turned up in a bag next to my gate because I first had to deal with the knowledge about muskrats that I subsequently gained from the Web. They are relatively harmless except they are known to damage dams and marinas and shorelines with their burrowing—which can be extensive. The picture of their burrows on the Web was unsettling, as was a little story in the paper that mentioned their having caused a flood by burrowing through a levee in Missouri. The only other thing I learned about them—which didn't seem relevant to my case at the time—is that they copulate while submerged, which I assume limits the time they can devote to foreplay since they can only stay underwater for twenty minutes.

And once I thoroughly understood their comfort in the water, I began to envision a brand-new threat to my yard and garden. What I had imagined as one or two muskrats became a big family in my mind's eye and I convinced myself that the riverbank-dwelling, tunnel-digging crew had created a burrow along the north border of my property with an entrance below the high-water line at the riverbank. That was a distance of twenty-five feet from the hole I could see. Much of that twenty-five-foot expanse was rock fill interspersed with the heavy roots of my ever-expanding fig tree. And the rock wall that covers my end of the burrow is made up of what may be one-man rocks for Dave my wall-builder but are two- or three-woman rocks as far as I'm concerned, especially in my ninth decade. Would I need to reconstruct the wall to eradicate the burrow?

I did rebuild another part of the riverbank myself twelve years ago, putting in hardware cloth to make sure the rocks didn't fall through to the beach and lining that with filter cloth so that the soil wouldn't wash into the river when the water came over the top. But the rocks in that crib were smaller, and I could handle them. The rocks in this wall were way too big for me. I wasn't sure I ever could have moved them, even twelve years ago; now I was certain I couldn't.

Why was it, I wondered, that the muskrats who had shared the river with me for thirteen-plus years waited until I was beginning to feel old, and had no man in the house to foist this job off on, to make a break for it? Their decision meant I had to try to coax the lovely man who built my wall into coming back for what amounted to a patch-up job—something he doesn't really enjoy doing. It also meant we'd have to put in hardware cloth to stop the muskrats from coming through again, and plastic to keep the river from leaking through, and I found myself wondering just how far Dave would have to dig to effectively barricade my riverbank. In any case, I really couldn't dump the kitty litter down the hole until I had called him, since making him dig through used kitty litter seemed distinctly unfriendly.

So I called Dave and, although I warned him of what he was in for, he came. Luckily, though, the burrow was nothing quite as I imagined. The tunnel went nowhere. And the hole that constituted the muskrats' den was just that—a hole. To get to it, Dave had to dig out a clump of irises. Then he lined the hole with chicken wire and plastic, rebuilt one end of the wall for what he reminded me was probably the third time (the other two were attempts to get it to stop leaking), and cleaned up everything just before a threatened snowstorm—which came as billed the next day, followed by an overnight freezing rain that put a hard crust on top.

A friend who knew the muskrat tale called the next morning and asked if I had been out to see whether there were any animal tracks. I hadn't been out, but decided I would go, just to check, although the path was covered with an unbroken expanse of snow and I didn't see any evidence of visitors.

When I walked down the path, I realized that the crust was so hard that a small animal running across it wouldn't even break it, so I wasn't going to find out much. But alas, I did. There at the same corner where the first pile of dirt had appeared was a swath of dirt on the snow, and leading in from it was a hole, behind the same rock wall that had just been rebuilt with fortifi-cations—and used kitty litter, which Dave scattered freely as he refilled the hole.

So I looked on the Web and learned that for twenty dollars I could get a month's supply of something called Critter Ridder, which seemed like over-expensive overkill. Looking further, I found and ordered a much cheaper small bottle of Muskrat Lure, which I planned to deploy in my next plan: setting the trap at the mouth of the hole, baiting it with the lure, and catching any muskrat in the vicinity well before there was anything pretty to eat on the riverbank.

Coexistence with Nature is certainly challenging.

CHAPTER SIXTEEN

Skunks on the Riverbank

Midway through the summer of 2009 I found myself transporting to a distant location the third skunk that had wandered that week into my Havahart trap. I was sick of skunks, really sick of them, despite the fact that when they're cleaned up, they're fluffy and beautiful. I hated the little holes they bored into the grass, I hated the fact that they dug up whatever vegetable scraps I buried to fertilize unused spaces in the garden, and that they made pits everywhere. But I hated them especially because they insisted on wandering into my Havahart trap set to catch the woodchuck, which was wreaking havoc on the brussels sprouts that were flourishing before his arrival. The prior year's crop had succumbed to an invasion of harlequin beetles; I was counting on this year's once giant, but now chomped plants to provide me with a generous winter crop.

I know I shouldn't complain. In a year when the whole Northeast had been suffering through the consequences of what may be the coolest, wettest summer ever, my tomato vines were red with fruit and I had begun to harvest my best-ever potato crop. I dug twenty-five pounds of lovely La Ratte fingerlings and fifteen pounds of the long-keeping Carola out of one three-by-fourteen bed, and I had just harvested the Russet Burbanks, which promised to weigh out in an equally generous manner. In the past too much water has often left me with potatoes that collapse in my hand as I pull them from the soil. Why I should have had such a triumphant year in the teeth of the wettest June on record is one of Nature's secrets.

I was humbly grateful, because my success had come in a summer when other farmers' crops had fallen to a version of the blight that long ago triggered the Irish potato famine. Here in the Northeast, the damned organisms took tomatoes first and overwhelmingly—*The New York Times* carried a picture of a farmer I know burying eight hundred of his blighted tomato plants—and then moved on to potatoes. These are folks for whom the summer tomato crop is often what stands between loss and profit on the farm. My farmer friend mowed down his potato tops and dug up his potatoes early, his wife told me by e-mail, hoping that the blight that was taking the plants hadn't yet affected the tubers.

I, on the other hand, had been going around bragging about my potato crop. "What will you do with all those potatoes?" one friend asked, thinking I guess of the hard time she has using up a ten-pound bag before the potatoes go limp. "Well, for one thing, I eat a lot of potatoes," I said. And I do, happily. The fact that my Russets came through that year—meaning I would have actual baking potatoes—made me happier than a mere vegetable should. Spuds are among my favorite vegetables, partly because I can store them to eat through the winter.

I store them on open shelves in boxes, each marked with the variety it contains, in what is supposed to be my cold cellar but hasn't worked out to be quite as cold as planned. It's a small space, superinsulated from the rest of the house and open to the elements through a small high window on the north wall that does not, as hoped, coax in the cold air.

I've tried to cool it with a fan on a thermostat and a fan without a thermostat, and I finally got someone to put a hole in the floor and run a stovepipe down to the basement where, presumably, the air is cooler so that if hot air is venting out the high window, cold air would theoretically be pulled up from the basement. Whatever. It's never worked really well, but I was able to keep my unexpectedly bountiful crop of potatoes, dutifully cleared of their sprouts from time to time, through May. Then I moved the best keepers to the refrigerator, where they lasted almost until the next season's potatoes began to produce tubers.

This was a good thing, since potatoes, white and sweet, are some of what I'll eat instead of brussels sprouts if I don't have any of the latter when winter comes. And since I eat, all through the year—fall, winter, spring, summer—only the vegetables I grow, the loss of a particular crop means the loss of a particular item in my yearly diet.

Which brings me back, indirectly enough, to the skunks. In years past, I had found someone who, for pay, would come and take away whoever got trapped in *my* yard to release into *her* yard. I was grateful to her, and even more grateful not to be one of her neighbors, since all that imported wildlife was surely wandering her neighborhood, dispersed by so much imported competition.

Now, I had always believed that the reason a skunk didn't let fly when you approached it in the trap was because that enclosed space prevented it from getting into attack mode. I figured it couldn't arch its back in there, and hold its tail forward over its head to spray. But when the animal-rescue lady coaxed the skunks she rescued into a four-foot-square cage whose ample dimensions would have readily permitted such a defensive posture, nothing happened as she carried them out and put them in her car.

Based on her bravado, I figured I could handle trapped skunks on my own. Still, I thought it wise to be cautious. And so the first time I caught one that I was relocating by myself, I approached it with a large piece of plastic, gingerly dropped it over the trap to conceal me and my captive from each other, gently took hold of the handle on top, and carried the trapped skunk out to my car, trying hard not to jar the trap or make any sudden moves.

It's worth noting here that skunks have the ability to dig three-inch-deep holes right through the wire floor of a trap, moving all the dirt inside. It's an astonishing skill, although I'm not inter-ested enough in how they do it to stand out there and watch. But what that ability means is that when you are carrying a skunk in a trap that you have incautiously set over a lawn or some other planted area, you will find yourself carrying the trap to your car lugging a small, lightweight skunk and ten pounds of dirt, and leaving behind you a pit or two and a totally torn-up rectangle of grass.

Which is what I had that morning in the wet, potato-and-tomato-blight summer when three skunks had ensconced themselves in my woodchuck trap in a single week: a dug-up patch of grass and a heavy dirt- and skunk-filled trap. And so I set off to repeat the journey I had made twice before that week, out across the county to a place where a broken-up macadam road leads to an empty house.

I used to go down the road, past the empty house, and release in privacy whatever I had come to release. But now the road was barred a few car lengths in. So I turned left at the light on the connecting road, went down the intersecting road for several hundred yards, to the turn-in marked DO NOT ENTER, and entered, feeling uneasy. I stopped my car, got out, opened the trunk, hoped no one was passing on the outer road, took out the trap, and set it on the ground. Then I removed the cover so I could see which way the skunk was facing, turned that end of the trap into the woods, opened the trap, and . . .

Nothing happened. Usually whoever is occupying the trap springs for freedom. But this skunk clung to the other end of the trap and wouldn't turn around. So I closed that end, turned the trap around, and opened the other end. The skunk had also turned around and was now at the other end. Someone pulled into the road and I tried not to notice that they were only fifteen feet behind me, watching. I had to get rid of the skunk. If whoever was watching wanted to arrest me, so be it. I lifted the end of the trap where the skunk was cowering and bounced it up and down, trying to dump him out. He clung to the little platform in the middle that triggers the trap when it's set. So I put the trap down, let him settle a little, then raised the closed end of the trap again and tried to dump him toward the open end. Finally he caught on and departed. So did the car behind me.

That problem was solved, but my underlying woodchuck problem was not. I realized that a woodchuck had taken up residence somewhere in my yard even before I saw him because of the successive dens he made trying to find a place to live that was handy to my broccoli. He had begun at the northern brussels sprouts bed where he dug a tremendous hole—throwing dirt everywhere— trying to get under my stone wall. I saw it while I was happily weeding listening to NPR's *Morning Edition* on my not up-to-date but cheap Walkman. But I was ready because I knew he was there. And I got one of the bags of used kitty litter I've kept handy for just such a purpose, dumped it down the hole, and with great effort, working through the cage that arcs the bed, filled everything in. Then I walked over to see how the onions were curing (it was July, time for them to dry off) and saw dirt on the path right next to the evergreens that separate my garden from the riverbank. My exclamation will not be written down, but it started with an *S* and ended with a *T*. A woodchuck had tried living there over a year earlier, digging two holes in succession, each of which I filled with used kitty litter, and that had ended it. I thought.

But when I lifted the juniper limbs, the new hole was enormous, and damn near inaccessible to someone who wasn't truly desperate to stop him. So I went and got my last bag of used kitty litter, propped up the limbs with a small ladder, and then decided I had to get in from the slightly higher riverbank. So I pushed past the branches, trying to forget I was eighty and often felt it, and climbed in with my Crocs slipping and poured in my bag of kitty litter. Then with my little aluminum trowel I pushed and shoved back into the hole as much as I could of the huge mound of dirt she had managed to excavate, tromped it down, added more kitty litter, pushed in more dirt (all of this while under attack by a very aggressive juniper), and climbed out through the juniper onto the path. There was a large rock I might have ruptured myself moving into the hole, but I figured the kitty litter would do it. And then it was 11 AM and I had come out at 6:30 intending to stay just an hour. So I went in for "breakfast" and took a nap. Sometime later, after cooking up the tomatoes as I promised myself, I went out and set the trap with broccoli and peanut butter.

And then, much later, I just happened to notice (I do think Mother Nature is helping me—these things keep "happening") that I could see the trap from the living room window and I got the binoculars (which I *never* use) to look and see whether or not the trap had been sprung. It hadn't. But I noticed something odd on the boardwalk. "I don't think I left anything there," I said to myself and looked more closely. A *woodchuck*. There it was, standing up, just looking around, probably plotting its next moves.

I went out on the terrace to see it better, watched for a while, and decided to go downstairs and creep quietly out onto the path to see if I could get close enough to see where he went. I did well. I got halfway out the path before the woodchuck realized something (or someone) was up, dropped to all fours, and started across the boardwalk, stopping halfway and then, as I kept walking, bolting toward the chain-link gate that separates my boardwalk from the one next door.

When I got out there, it was clear that there was nowhere for my woodchuck to have gone except next door. She must have climbed around the gate and onto the neighbor's dock, despite the chicken wire I had strung there previously to try to prevent such cross-border invasions. So I fiddled with the chicken wire for a while, and made a mental note to get more the next day. But then I had a new problem: I was going to fortify my fence, but I needed to make sure the woodchuck was out of the yard before I strung the new wire. So I set the trap again, and hoped he took the broccoli and peanut butter before another skunk beat him to it.

Alas, another skunk did, so I took him out and dumped him in the usual place, and when I came back with the trap, I discovered that the woodchuck had been busy again, this time digging not one but two holes in my wall in another vain attempt to get through to the other side. How he did it is a mystery since he dug through a bed filled with chicken wire added when I was having the (sigh) muskrat problems. So I set the trap again, and next morning I looked to see what I had caught in my trap baited with lettuce and cucumber (suggested on the Web as woodchuck delights). Nothing, not even a skunk.

The next night I added two green beans with a lot of peanut butter to the tray of goodies. And the next morning I went out and found two green beans, no peanut butter, and the trap unsprung. But as I walked out to the path, I realized the woodchuck had clambered up the chicken wire and eaten the tops off my soybeans. Arrgh! So I went and got floating row covers and wrapped the whole package, sides and top. Someone had told me that a woodchuck wouldn't go after what he could not see.

At this point, the woodchuck was also topping off each broccoli plant as it came into bud. So I decided to get out some netting to cover the broccoli bed that was just about ready to harvest. It took a while, but I did it, taking advantage of the opportunity to cut back the snapped-off (and eaten-off) broccoli to a short stalk with only two leaves and thus collecting a lot of broccoli litter, and as I was about to do the next broccoli bed, I decided that what I really wanted to protect instead was my brussels sprouts bed. He had only hit that once, and the plants looked too wonderful to be wiped out.

So I netted that bed too, and when I looked at my watch I realized that, once again, it was now late morning. I was feeling pretty miffed by the fact that I was spending so much of my gardening time protecting the produce. But then I reminded myself that I had tomatoes and potatoes already harvested and that was not to be sneezed at in this year of the Irish blight.

Since I had nothing else to do with the broccoli litter, I put a lot of it into the trap, some at the entrance, some inside leading to the little platform. And the next morning, I was sufficiently wood-

chuck-burned to not bother going out until a couple of my gradu-
ate students arrived, very late, around eleven thirty, to help in the
garden. I described my animal problems to them as we walked
outside. I had left the trap covered with burlap, and when we
reached it we could see that it had been sprung but couldn't see
what was in it. I pulled back the burlap expecting another skunk.
But there was the *woodchuck*. I don't think my migrant laborers
could believe the extremity of my delight, but then, of course,
they had not shared the extremity of my vegetal frustration.

So we took the woodchuck over to its disposal place, opened
the trap, and the most amazing thing happened. As expected, he
leaped from the trap and scurried into the woods. But then, even
before we got back into the car, he dashed back out of the woods,
ran under the car, and sped into the woods on the other side. And
after we got into the car, we saw him charging up the road beyond
the barrier faster than I had ever seen a woodchuck move. Clearly
there was something in the woods he didn't want to encounter.

Two days later I was out weeding where the front of my house
meets the street, and a friend from the community garden came
by. I told her I had caught our neighborhood woodchuck and,
pleased, she asked where I took the garden visitors to let them
go. As I described the place, she said, "Oh, I know that place. I
pass it every day going to work. There's a red fox hanging out
there. I've seen him several times." She said he was beautiful and
would stand there right where I parked. And then she mentioned
that red foxes smelled slightly skunky.

So now we know. I'm sure the woodchuck smelled the fox—
sensing the subtle difference between being a skunk and smell-
ing like you eat skunks—and took off, figuring that foxes smart
enough to eat skunks also knew how to eat woodchucks. And
I've been feeding that fox a breakfast skunk every morning. No
wonder he hangs around. Probably stays right there and waits for
my next arrival!

How's that for working with Nature?

CHAPTER SEVENTEEN

The Maple Tree

I have a splendid maple tree in my yard towering over the ever-greens that hold the territory close to the house. It provides shade to my terrace in the summer, and beauty to the garden all year long—a massive leafy assertion on a thirty-six-foot-wide village lot. The tree is well over fifty feet tall, and still growing, its swelling trunk now wedged hard against the stockade fence erected five years ago a half foot away. I anticipate major fence surgery one day soon, a possibility I view benignly. The tree was here first, after all. I love it and would miss it powerfully should it ever attract an Asian longhorned beetle, like those now killing the trees of New York City. I have no idea what its ecological role is in the eight thousand square feet of land I have taken responsibility for, but I have no doubt that it has one.

Despite my profound affection for this giant, however, there are a couple of months in spring when I harbor serious thoughts of arboricide. On this May morning, for example, I was out with a Shop-Vac, sucking up the hundreds of maple keys trapped in the cracks between the boards of my deck, when I realized that I would do almost anything to keep this massive fellow organism from taking so enthusiastically to reproduction. In early spring, just as the garden begins to shake off the effects of winter and send out its tenderly beautiful green shoots, the maple bursts into flower, flinging its sex in every direction, causing my nose to itch, my eyes to water, and, shortly after, pelting the yard with its little tassels of pollen. These rapidly coalesce into a sullen sludge, and as the droppings rot in the corners of the terrace under the March rains, they coat the floor with what morphs into a kind of black paste. I dig the goo out of the corners, scrub off the black coating it has left on the terra-cotta-colored terrace floor, and take a deep breath.

Then comes late May, and the winged progeny of the pollen barrage come pelting to earth, covering everything within a fifty-foot radius of the tree trunk with a heavy layer of potential maple seedlings and thoroughly trashing my yard. I don't want to seem hypercritical, but there are literally thousands of them. The terrace is once more inundated, chairs, table, the orange and lime trees that have just been moved outdoors for the summer, thousands and thousands of winged seeds, whirling down from the tree like miniature helicopters.

In a good year we may have heavy winds around this time, bringing most of the sailers down from the tree in a rush, sending most of the maple babes voyaging off south—enraging the community gardeners next door, but reducing my cleanups to one or two. When we have drenching rains they wash many of the spinners down to the ground from the place where they first landed. But alas, there are always enough thousands noticeably left around to make cleaning them up essential. This task includes not only sweeping down the terrace and vacuuming the deck, but painstakingly picking the youngsters off the creeping thyme, a task that cannot—I have learned from painful experience—be done with a vacuum, or even with a broom.

What is it with maple seeds? Why are there so many of them? They seem to germinate so easily and successfully that there is concern in the Northeast about the fact that invader red maples are crowding out the natives in our woods. I can't imagine that there's much of a call for maple seeds, because a maple isn't a marigold that needs to set seed every year in order to carry on the family tree (if you'll pardon the pun). Maples don't die each winter—they only drop their leaves—which are, by the way, remarkably easy to deal with compared with the oak leaves I had to clean up where I lived before.

So it's only the reproductive enthusiasm of maples that bothers me. How many times, after all, do you need to start a new maple from seed? (I forgot to mention that many of those adorable little fliers do try to grow, so one spends many June afternoons pulling up incipient maples.) And so, as I stood vacuuming my deck, I realized that at this time of year I can sympathize with the technologists' desire to mold Nature not just to our necessity, but to our convenience; I can empathize with my species' temptation to try to bring under control all the parts of Nature that don't suit us.

I really don't want the maple neutered. That's the trick being tried out by the giant companies that are coming increasingly to control our seed supply—inserting what critics have dubbed "terminator" genes into plants so they will set sterile seeds. I find such an intervention appalling—one more fatal step in our belief that we can turn everything we touch into gold, without starving to death as King Midas did when he was granted that wish. And they're doing it with crops that do have to be planted every year, not with trees like my maple that can count their life spans in decades.

So I don't wish sterility on my maple; I've just found myself wondering if we couldn't make it a little less spendthrift, a little more "efficient." It is surely wasteful for Nature to produce so many maple keys. It takes energy to produce all that pollen and all those seeds, only to have them swept up and carted away by irate homeowners.

The urge to control Nature probably wasn't innate for our species, since hunters and gatherers were happy eating whatever Nature provided. But when we discovered agriculture, we really bought in to the idea of "control." I became aware of the power of this urge years ago when I saw my pepper plants flourishing in one bed, and shrinking in another. Reflecting on this inexplicable occurrence, I understood how tempting it must have been to try to eliminate that variety, to buy in to the idea that we could bring Nature to the kind of uniformity machines have accomplished in other aspects of our lives. Biotech is simply the latest of these efforts, and the inventors of this new technique once again assure us that "This time we've got it right."

Alas, there's no guarantee of that, and the consequences of their being wrong could be literally deadly. I keep tacked to my computer a quotation of the day from a copy of *The New York Times*. The quotee is president and owner of Prairie State Semen in Illinois, commenting on the fact that the Food and Drug Administration has just declared cloned animals safe for the food supply. "When you buy a box of Cheerios in New York and one in Champaign, Illinois," he said, "you know they are going to be the same. By shortening the genetic pool using clones, you can do a similar thing." Remarkable! A Cheerio Cow. Given the alternative, I think I'll just hang in there with my maple tree and its splendidly spendthrift sexual habits.

CHAPTER EIGHTEEN

Zucchini (Warning: Contains Recipes)

It is a fact I don't often admit that I am sometimes more interested in the beauty of the garden than in the fact that it feeds me. I know this because given a choice of tasks, I will almost inevitably choose beautifying over harvesting. Sometimes I stay outside so long working on tidying up the garden that I don't even have the energy to cook what I have produced. I miss Alan at these times, since he never allowed himself to get carried away by work, and always started dinner if it was time. With me, there is always a contest—as there is with many gardeners, I suspect—between abundance and control. In the vegetable garden this is illustrated most vividly, perhaps, by zucchini, the plant you can never grow just enough of.

Until I grew Costata Romanesca (about which my seed catalog remarks, "This is the only zucchini to grow unless you like water"), my yearly love affair with zucchini was always brief. Some time in late May or early June when the danger of frost was reliably past, Alan would pick a bed where we had not planted zucchini in several years, deeply dig two or three circles maybe a foot and a half in diameter and six inches apart, and fork in manure and compost, plus a small handful of a bonemeal, blood meal, and greensand mix. Then he would use his index finger to poke three or four shallow holes around the outside, two or three inches in from the edge of the circle, drop a couple of seeds in each, fill the holes with dirt rubbed between his hands to make it fine, and water down the area.

Some days later—depending on the temperature—the hulking seedlings would shoulder their way to the surface, first pushing their humped stems out of the ground, then straightening up to wrench their giant seed leaves out of the soil and up to the sun. Usually all of them came up, two from a hole, eight from a circle, twenty-four in the bed. Then I would begin the battle to make Alan pull most of them out to leave room for the giant plants they would become. Usually he objected, and left several more plants than we needed, so we always had more zucchini than we could eat.

The first flowers were the useless males, lots of them. I intend no sexual commentary here; it's simply a fact that until a flower bud emerges with a bulge at its stem end to demonstrate its femininity, the male flowers are—from the standpoint of a squash eater—pointless. I willingly acknowledge here that their deeper purpose may be to lure a crowd of bees with the information "Pollen here! Pollen here!" so that when the female flowers open, there will be a glut of pollinators. And of course the males can be deliciously stuffed, battered and fried, but if you're waiting for zucchini, those boy flowers don't count.

Finally, a female bud emerges, enlarges, and opens. After which, quicker than you expect, a slender green squash awaits your morning walk. But only briefly. Go away for a weekend, or stay inside for a day or two of rain, and the petite and tender fruit has swelled up into a squash as big as your forearm. A day or two later there's nothing to be done but cut the monster from the vine and sneak it into someone's unlocked car. And a few weeks later, of course, the plants collapse, victims of squash vine borers.

But my worst problem with zucchini has never been their tendency to over-reproduce, bloat, and die. It's that most of the good recipes I have for this particular squash say "brown the slices," and that's simply ridiculous. Put slices of your ordinary zucchini in a frying pan with olive oil and their pores open, spilling out enough water to eliminate any possibility of browning.

So when I found—well into my life of zucchini growing—a recipe that overcame the water problem, I was ecstatic. The secret is to cut it in julienne strips. So for those of you stuck with ordinary zucchini, here it is. It's delicious.

ZUCCHINI WITH OIL AND LEMON

Trim off the ends of
2–3 **zucchini** (about 1¼ pounds) and cut
into julienne strips about 2 inches long.

Now heat in a large skillet
3 tablespoons **olive oil**.

Add the zucchini, **salt**, and freshly ground **pepper**
to taste. Cook, stirring, until the zucchini starts to
brown.
(It will, it will!)

Add
juice of ½ lemon.
Cover and cook for about 3 minutes more, until
the squash is crisp and slightly browned. Serve
immediately.

I deduced that the reason one can brown julienned zucchini and not zucchini slices is because the channels that carry fluid from the base of the fruit to its tip run up and down, so when you cut them across all the water leaks out—but when you cut them vertically, only the little cut ends leak. Voilà! Browning.

But there is another, even more satisfactory, solution to the water problem—Costata Romanesca, which you can cut up any way you like. Not only that, the fruits are beautiful—dark and lighter green, heavily ribbed and slightly twisted. And when they get big, even really big, you can still use them. Indeed, you can leave a foot-long squash on the kitchen counter for a week and it won't get soft or spoil; when you cut it, it will still be tender from the skin in. My next-door community gardeners love the fruits but won't grow them because the plants are so huge, they take up half of a nine-by-ten plot! Gigantism is apparently what allows them to tough out the unfailing borer attack, though they get to looking pretty bad as their older leaves collapse.

If you're fortunate enough to have a garden big enough to grow these gentle giants, you will discover that the catalog is right. Costata can be sliced, cubed, or even shredded without presenting you with a pan of water. Which means it can be used in a recipe like the following—and that when you arrive for dinner carrying a two-pound fruit, everyone will smile.

SQUASH WITH MUSHROOMS
adapted from Diana Kennedy

Rinse, trim, and cut into ¼-inch cubes
　　2 medium **zucchini** (about 1 pound).
In a small sauté pan, heat
　　2 tablespoons **vegetable oil**—or less.

Add
　　2½ tablespoons finely chopped **white onion**
　　1 **poblano chili**, charred, peeled, and cut
　　into narrow strips
　　sprinkle of **salt**.
Cook uncovered, without browning, for 1 minute.

Add
squash cubes.
Cover the pan and cook over medium heat, shaking the pan from time to time to prevent sticking.
Cook for 10 minutes or until the squash is tender.

Meanwhile, in a separate skillet, toss
½ pound **shiitake mushrooms** in
1 tablespoon **oil**. Sprinkle with **salt**.
Stir-fry for 5 minutes or until the juice becomes almost gelatinous.

Add the mushrooms to the squash mix.

Sprinkle the top of the vegetables with
½ cup roughly chopped **cilantro**.

Dot with
½ cup plain **yogurt** and top with
2–3 slices **provolone** with
¼ cup **grated cheddar** on top of them.
Cover the pan and cook over gentle heat for 5 minutes or until the cheese has melted. Serve in warm corn tortillas.

Zucchini is perhaps the ideal poster child for the fact that limitations produce creativity. And because I'm so thrilled to have solved the water problem, I've included several recipes in this chapter. There are thousands of recipes for zucchini. I even have one that uses giant oblong zucchini slices as pizza bases.

I once taught a month-long course in Japan designed for Japanese students earning a degree in English as a Second Language. Because of my interest in environmentally responsible eating, I got in touch with an organization I had heard of called the Seikatsu Club. This was a group of Japanese women who, having banded together to get cheaper milk, ended up becoming an influential food cooperative that put consumers in touch with food producers. Not only did they purchase fruits and vegetables directly from small farmers, but in a country that was in trouble internationally for pillaging the oceans of seafood, the Seikatsu Club made a point of purchasing only sustainably produced fish and shellfish.

I was deeply impressed by what they had accomplished. And as a longtime critic of the bloated American supermarket where the number of choices offered has overwhelmed shoppers' choice-making capacity, I was impressed by one of the Seikatsu club principles. They did not make pre-prepared salad dressing because they believed that having too many foods premade stifled creativity.

I am convinced by my own experience that such is the case. The longer I spend using only the fruits and vegetables that I can grow, the more inventive I become at finding ways to use them. And I am not alone in this. A dear friend who also grows her family's food once sent me a recipe I call Invisible Zucchini that might never have been invented if it hadn't been for squash overwhelm.

BARBARA K'S INVISIBLE ZUCCHINI

Coarsely grate
   4 **zucchini** (or one large one!).
Salt and let sit for 20 minutes in a colander to drain. Squeeze dry.

Combine in a blender
   2 big handfuls **basil**

2 cloves **garlic**
¼–½ cup **olive oil**.
Puree.

Meanwhile, cook for 6 minutes
¾ cup **orzo**.

Toss everything together and, while it's still hot, add
4 ounces (about ½ cup) freshly grated **Parmesan cheese**.

Serve warm or room temperature.

In order to have this delicious recipe in the winter, I shred some of my giant zucchini, sauté the shreds briefly in butter, spread the product on a cookie sheet, and freeze it. When it is frozen, I break it up with a cleaver and store the pieces in a freezer bag. Since I also freeze pesto base (everything but the butter and the cheese) in ice cube trays, I can make this wonderful dish in winter and spring when other fresh-tasting things are absent from the garden.

I have even found a way to control the sprawl of the humongous plants that produce these squash, which do not shy from sending out a stalk eighteen inches long topped by a leaf the size of a turkey platter. Control is a necessity in a garden as small as mine since even two of these plants do not take kindly to being confined in a single bed three feet wide and fifteen feet long. They rapidly push out across the paths on either side of the bed and have to be gently lifted back in and restrained with a stick inserted into the soil. Then one year I came up with a new plan—plant zucchini in one of the alfalfa beds.

I had previously planted two of my garden beds to alfalfa,

partly because I thought it would give the bed a rest—alfalfa being a nitrogen fixer—and partly because I thought my soil in general was running down and I should start building it up by cutting alfalfa and mixing it in with the compost. It seemed a good idea, but it didn't work out. When the alfalfa was readiest to be cut, the garden was madly producing green matter and had no need of this extra dose of nitrogenous materials. What I needed in summer was brown matter, sources of carbon. And in the fall and winter, when I had abundant carbon materials, the alfalfa was dormant.

But since the remaining beds were producing more food than I could eat or give away, I just left these two in alfalfa, cutting the stalks back once in a while to use their greenery for mulch, and then, every fall, mowing the beds to give the plants a fresh start. A couple of years ago in spring, looking for a home for the long-legged kale plants that had wintered over, I transplanted two tall kales into one of the alfalfa beds. The alfalfa helped screen the naked kale stems, and the kale filled in a couple of holes in the alfalfa bed. Then one year I had an inspiration. If I put the zucchini in the alfalfa bed, the vigorously growing alfalfa would help confine the zucchini as well as conceal the soil-level mess of ruined stalks and yellowed leaves that charted the borers' progress up their woody stems. Except for the fact that the zucchini appeared to have smothered much of the alfalfa by fall, this particular experiment was a blazing success.

ZUCCHINI PANCAKES WITH
GOLDEN TOMATO CONCASSE
from Jessie Cool

Skin, seed, and chop coarsely
   1 pound **golden tomatoes**.
Let them drain in a colander.

Meanwhile, grate
     1½ pounds **zucchini**
     1 medium **red onion**.
Sprinkle with **salt**.

Let stand for 10 minutes, squeeze out the excess
water, and combine with
     2 cloves **garlic**, crushed
     2 tablespoons chopped fresh **mint** or **basil**
     ⅛ teaspoon ground **nutmeg**
     2 tablespoons grated **Parmesan cheese**
     2 **eggs**, beaten
     3 tablespoons unbleached **white flour**
     pinch of freshly ground **black pepper**.

In a heavy-bottomed skillet, heat ¼ inch of **canola oil** until smoking.

Drop in ¼ cup of zucchini batter, flattening if necessary. Flip when thoroughly brown.

Serve with chopped yellow tomato on top of or under zucchini pancake.

This zucchini commentary might have ended right there were it not for an accident that happened as I wrote this. After years of making compost from my garbage mixed with all the chopped-up leafy and woody materials in my yard, I concluded that in the absence of manure, I was not happy with the outcome and would, for at least one summer, try simply burying my wet garbage in beds from which I had harvested potatoes or onions. All the woody material would be chopped and put on top of the beds for mulch. So one day in September when my back was turned, a zucchini came up out of one of the garbaged beds, undoubtedly a spawn of Costata.

But if Costata was oversized, this plant was downright scary. I can assert without exaggeration that it spread three feet wide across the bed in one weekend. I came home from being away and there it was. A visitor who came by at the time looked at me oddly and muttered something about "Little Shop of Horrors." And I found myself imagining that this plant was shouting to me "See, if you feed me right, this is what I can do!" In a day or two it set two zucchini fruits—giant fruits, looking something like the water bottles long-distance bicyclists carry, fully two inches in diameter and almost a foot long.

Costata have, as I said, quite beautiful fruit, ribbed and slightly twisted. This plant was having nothing of such refinement. This was a throwback to something primitive, and not to be toyed with. As it continued throwing off fruits even as October's end had laid frost on most people's lawns, I found myself relieved that it had come up in the fall. I would find it hard to kill a plant that was trying so hard, and was comforted to know that Nature would soon do it for me!

CHAPTER NINETEEN

Bees

I'm fairly certain that I've worried longer about bees than most people who don't actually keep hives or study insects for a living. I've been uttering Cassandra-like warnings about the vulnerability of honeybees to pesticides for thirty years at least, but I don't think I really *got* it until a particular June morning more than a decade ago when Alan was still alive. I was taking a very early walk in the garden as I do at the least opportunity on the long June days leading up to the solstice. I stopped at each bed, pulling weed seedlings in one, leading a bean tendril to its climbing pole in another. A giant zucchini plant tumbled out of one of the beds, sprawling over the path, its flamboyant yellow-orange flowers gaping to welcome their pollinators.

And, surprised by an unusual lack of activity, I suddenly remembered that that summer no honeybees were likely to arrive for an embrace by these lascivious blossoms. In a recent Sunday paper, the garden writer had reported that New York's honeybee colonies, already reduced from more than two hundred thousand after World War II to less than a quarter of that, had succumbed in horrifying numbers to the year's hard winter. The season's record snows were apparently not their only problem. The bees were weakened by parasitic mites, and—after a dry fall—had been short of honey going into what turned out to be a long cold winter. A local beekeeper was quoted as saying that 50 to 80 percent of his hives were dead.

I wasn't entirely surprised. During the 1980s, I was on a sustainable agriculture listserv that very often alerted me to things I never dreamed I would need to know about. Warnings of coming honey shortages and of the spread of two kinds of bee mites (varroa and tracheal) had appeared in recent weeks. So the garden writer's story, emerging briefly from the daily fire-hose of information that threatens to drown us all, hadn't really jolted me. Now, in the garden, the reality of the loss made me stop short. The warm buzzing that should have been part of the morning's background wasn't there.

I looked around. Instead of nodding collectively under the weight of bees, the lavender blossoms stood erect, quivering occasionally at the landing of a solitary insect. Walking down the brick paths between the vegetable beds, I didn't have to push carefully by umbels of flowering coriander bent into the path by eager foragers. No small bodies hummingly bumped my arms as I reached in to tug a weed from the alyssum patch. I'm not bee-sensitive. I have always walked and worked among them with-out concern, brushing them aside when they're busy in a place I need to be, as they often are . . . or used to be.

My husband, who was alive then for what we did not know would be his last summer, called a local apple farmer who keeps hives to pollinate his crops. His apples had been fertilized, and he didn't plan to rent his hives. Then Alan called the local Cooperative Extension Service to locate a hive we might rent for our crops and those in the community garden next door. We spoke on the phone to the local beekeeper whom the service recommended—the one quoted in the newspaper—and he came to see us the next day. The year before, he had set out more than thirty hives around the county, he said. All of them were dead. Now he had brought six fresh ones up from the South. He told us that when he got our call, he had contacted his Georgia supplier to see if they would send another hive. They refused to send any more bees through the Chicago airport, because, to be safe, the Chicago mail minders had shrink-wrapped his last mailing, bees and all!

And he wasn't sure he dared risk relocating one of his own new hives to our land; the bees might not have enough nectar sources to lay down their winter stores. But he agreed to think about it. Of all the people Alan and I had spoken to about the bee disappearance, he was the only one who expressed any serious concern. It was not other people's disinterest that surprised me most, however, but my own prior inattention. Most folks are sufficiently removed from the land to have forgotten the importance of bees, but I spend a lot of time in the garden now that I am semi-retired.

Thirty years ago I had unexpectedly learned something about loss after spending the late nights of the same deliciously elongating pre-solstice days working on a review of the candy industry for my father-in-law. The candy trade paper he published was celebrating its twenty-fifth anniversary, and he thought he would give his ex-reporter daughter-in-law a little something professional to do. He had not counted on my compulsiveness—honed by years as a *Time* magazine researcher. If I was going to write *Candy Industry*'s history, I was bound to at least *glance* through every issue. It was deadly work—ancient moldy-in-a-fortnight insider news about an industry in which I had, if anything, a negative interest. I was not yet a nutritionist by profession, but I *was* concerned with healthful eating. Candy did not rank high on my preferred food list.

I bring up this painful story now because managing my father-in-law's assignment, with two young sons and a stay-at-home artist husband, required me to do most of my concentrating at night. Toward the end, when my failure to finish would have wrecked our family vacation, I stayed up pretty late. And I remember panicking when I would hear the first scattered calls of the noisy bird chorus that indicated the imminent arrival of dawn. The sound would rise and rise in waves—screams, whistles, cries, peeps, caws, trills, as if every bird in the neighborhood were joining in to welcome the sun. The birds warned me that the man and boys would be up soon; once again before I had finished my writing work.

And then I got older, and so did my children. I went back to school to get a degree so I would no longer need to accept any more writing assignments from men, and ended up as a very busy professor of nutrition education. And one spring morning when, unusually, I had a few minutes to lie in bed after I woke, I noticed suddenly that there was no bird chorus. I had no idea how long it had been gone.

By now I was depressing students every fall, telling them about human-induced threats to the biosphere, including the threat to songbirds posed by the disappearance of their winter roosts in Central and South American forests. Yet I had never noticed that in my own world, much of the spring's morning chorus was silent. Twenty years later the morning of the absent bees reminded me that I hadn't missed the absent birds for a long, long time. Which is how it is when we self-absorbed humans change the sensory world around us. We are too busy to notice what used to be; our children will never know what they missed.

One more ancient tale. In my book *The Feeding Web,* published twenty-plus years ago, I wrote the following bee story, trying to explain how everything is connected:

> Some time ago a method was developed of encapsulating a highly toxic pesticide (parathion) in a time-release capsule. No pesticide was released as long as it was in solution, as it was while being applied. Only when the capsule got onto the plant and dried off was the pesticide released. This was very good for the agricultural workers. Unfortunately for the bees, the capsules turned out to be about the same size as pollen grains, so they adhered to foraging bees, who carried them back to the hives and promptly wiped them out. When a local specialist was contacted by the bee-owners, his memorable comment was that the bees were "trespassing" on the sprayed orchards.

I went on,

> Teaching a bee not to trespass surely presents a signifi-
> cant technological challenge. With any luck, we will meet
> that challenge before the bees are wiped out. But we had
> better hurry. Pesticide "accidents" have already caused
> a striking loss in bee colonies throughout the country,
> and especially in California. And bees—as those of us
> who remember our sex education will recall—are still
> required to fertilize everything from almond orchards
> to hybrid soybeans.

Because I am a born optimist, I keep thinking that my fellow
humans will learn not to continue doing things that are iden-
tifiably stupid. So for some years after I read that story about
encapsulated pesticides, I assumed that the comment about tres-
passing bees was merely one person's casually bizarre opinion.
But as it so often does, reality exceeded my wildest expectations.
Ten years later the *Maryland Pesticide Applicator Manual* contained
the following helpful information:

> If bees in hives are killed as the result of drift, the
> applicator is held legally responsible and often must
> pay damages. If bees contacted the pesticide in sprayed
> fields, the applicator usually is not liable; the courts have
> ruled that the bee is trespassing and that the land does
> not need to be safe for uninvited animals.

When I told that story to my older son, he said with delicious
irony, "Well, Mom, if animals have rights, they also have respon-
sibilities—you can't let bees be irresponsible." Then we laugh-
ingly made up a new product slogan—"This honey comes from
responsible bees."

Sometimes, out of necessity, bees are invited to trespass. When

I was in Alaska in the early 1970s, I learned that California was importing Alaskan bees to pollinate the state's food crops. So few crops were grown in Alaska, and for such a short season, that its environment, unlike California's, was relatively pest- and hence pesticide-free. So Alaskans shipped their bees south to do their thing in California's fields.

Their thing—the thing that bees and other pollinators do—is a detailed and time-consuming task: flying from flower to flower to collect nectar and, in the process, move pollen from stamens to pistils, from male to female plant parts, so a plant can bring to maturity whatever "fruit" that plant produces—almonds, oranges, peppers, buckwheat. It is a job for which humans are so ill equipped that it has always been difficult for me to imagine how bees might be replaced by human invention.

Most of the "advances" in agriculture—pesticides, herbicides, synthetic fertilizers—have been ways of substituting things made directly or indirectly from petroleum for things Nature normally takes care of: fertilizers for soil fertility, pesticides for insect control, herbicides for weed control. But whatever might we substitute to carry out the task of pollination? Oddly enough, there's now an answer.

Several years ago, in a report from the Center for Health and the Global Environment of the Harvard Medical School, a chapter on "Ecosystem Services" opened with a picture of two young women—Nepalese women, the caption indicated—hand pollinating a blooming apple tree.

> Bees in Maoxian County at the border between China and Nepal have gone extinct, forcing people to pollinate apple trees by hand. It takes 20 to 25 people to pollinate 100 trees, a task that can be performed by 2 bee colonies.[18]

So it's finally been demonstrated, experimentally so to speak, that bees are stunningly more efficient than people, and there is no reasonable substitute, a fact that urgently needs acting on before it's too late.

Not *everything* we eat depends on bees. Our local beekeeper told me that peas and beans are pretty well self-pollinating, but anything bees hang around a lot probably depends on them. The most commonly cited statistic is that about a third of what we eat is directly or indirectly pollinated by honeybees. So I suppose we could survive even if we killed them off, but we would notice the loss—of fruit, for example, and of almonds. In spring half of all the beehives in the nation are brought in to pollinate the California almond crop, which represents a staggering 80 percent of the *world's* almond production.[19] It's probably not particularly good for the bees to be moved around so much—nor to be put on a one-item diet of almond nectar. And it may be those stresses, along with the mites and pesticides, that are causing bee death.

Leaving aside the things we eat, the loss of the pollinators of the great majority of the plant world that we don't eat could well threaten the survival of life. For once I became aware of the decline of the bees, I learned that this is only part of a more general loss of pollinators—bees, wasps, butterflies. This pollinator crisis, it has been argued,[20] may be the most serious threat yet to the ecological systems that sustain us. A book called *The Forgotten Pollinators* taught me another surprising fact—that our honeybees are actually European imports, so "efficient" (a favorite American word) at foraging that they have displaced many of the native pollinators that used to fertilize plants before the immigrant bees arrived.

But now that disease and parasites are taking the honeybees, the native pollinators may have begun to resurge, so I've been watching carefully to see who is doing the pollinating in my garden. There are bigger bees with black bodies, and wasps, and tiny little flies, and lots of butterflies on the stiff orange tithonia flowers. And someone has pollinated the melons, although the cucumbers are sparse.

You can coax some pollinators into your garden by giving them little houses—orchard mason bees can apparently be lured to make their nests in blocks of wood with rows of holes bored into them. However, despite their name, these bees don't get up early enough in the year to be out pollinating when the early fruit trees are blooming, so they probably can't manage the whole job. Surprisingly, orchard bees are very reluctant to sting—*gentle* is the word used to describe them—but it's likely to be hard to convince non-gardeners of bee gentleness. Stinging is what most people think bees do.

This means that from the standpoint of humans who aren't growing anything, bees—all bees—probably seem more of a nuisance than anything else, and dangerous, as they probably seemed to the Chicago post office that shrink-wrapped them. Once, in a workshop about peace, I moderated a session titled "Peas and Peace" in which I compared modern farming's relationship to Nature with our nation's relationship to the Soviet Union—once a threat, I should explain to those of you attaining adulthood since its breakup. Feeling attacked by weeds, bugs, uncertain weather, we arm ourselves with heavy weapons as we did during the Cold War. Then in the garden, we hunker down and fire them.

In preparing the audience for my screed, I gave them a questionnaire to provoke their thinking. One of the questions was "A wasp is buzzing around your head examining you. What do you do?" When we discussed their answers, almost no one reported that they would just stand quietly and let the wasp reconnoiter. To a person, their perception was that a close-in flying organism—especially one with a stinger—was dangerous and should provoke some dramatic gesture, if only running away.

Recently, when I remarked to several people who were trying to get a local builder to "resod" his lawn that he should just add to the clover that has already begun to take over, they told me that builders don't plant clover.

Why? I said.

Clover flowers attract bees.

So? I asked.

Well, people worry about bees.

Why?

Well, they're afraid for their children.

Why?

Bees sting.

Only if you flail around when they come close or walk on them barefoot.

Well . . .

My path down to the river is mostly clover, but there are few bees on it anymore, so maybe builders can use clover now. Except, because everything is connected, producing clover seed requires that bees pollinate the clover flowers, so the seed may either have to be imported or awfully expensive, or both.

Where food is concerned, however, we can't be so cavalier. For instance, bees fertilize the high-protein alfalfa, red clover, trefoil, and other legumes that make much of our beef and milk production possible, and, as I said earlier, we would lose a lot of our other favorite foods if we lost bees. So trying to save the honeybees becomes one more argument for markedly reducing pesticides, retaining a greater diversity of plants in the fields to keep the bees' diets healthy, and generally encouraging many of the practices that a sustainable local food system implies.

However, as I have tried in the course of my professional lifetime to teach various audiences about the inescapable interconnectedness of humanity and the natural world, I have been repeatedly reminded that such an understanding does not come easily. To make clear our dependence on species and processes not under our control, I often use biologist Paul Ehrlich's short and simple list of the things Nature regulates as a matter of course, what he calls Nature's free services:

Maintenance of the gaseous quality of the atmosphere, amelioration of climate, operation of the hydrologic cycle (including the control of floods and the provision of fresh water to agriculture, industry and homes), disposal of wastes, recycling of the nutrients essential to agriculture and forestry, generation of soils, pollination of crops, provision of food from the sea, and maintenance of a vast genetic library from which humanity has already drawn the very basis of its civilization.[21]

Ehrlich's reference to crop pollination is what brought up the notion of free services, since the work of bees is a particularly vivid example of Nature's largely unrecognized contributions to our survival. The busyness of bees going about their life task is just one of the things that Nature now arranges without our attention—so long as we don't interfere too much. Which is why I keep updating myself on bees—because pollination is such a notable example of one of Nature's free services we would not want to do without.

So I've been startled and alarmed as the Chinese have moved in to dominate the honey market in recent years. Those women pollinators on China's border make it reasonable to ask whether China will be able to continue as a reliable source of cheap honey. Given the level of pollution there, it may be only a matter of time before there are a lot of women pollinating. And women pollinators don't produce honey—or beeswax—as they work. Which only goes to show that if things get bad enough, even our choice of sweeteners will be affected. It would be nice to think people would notice, but since most of what's on the supermarket shelves has only the most tenuous connection with Nature, it has seemed unlikely that the disappearance of a few products would alert ordinary consumers to the biological collapse of the world outside the store.

With all the ongoing stresses, Nature threw us something new a couple of years ago. Suddenly the bees were not visibly dying—they were simply disappearing. The "disease," if that's the right word, was called Colony Collapse Disorder (CCD)—a name that, like the physician's announcement "it's a virus," accurately suggested that no one knew what was causing the problem. One Cornell University entomologist noted that the actual causes were unknown although genetically modified foods, mites, pathogens, pesticides, and electromagnetic radiation from cell phones had all been proposed. In other words, the bees' environment—and ours?—is multiply hostile. Disturbingly, the bees were not coming back from foraging to die in the hives; they were simply disappearing, unable, unwilling, to find their way home.

After a couple of terrifying years, CCD itself seemed to wane in some parts of the world as mysteriously as it had waxed, but there were reports that 2009 was the worst year yet. And there is a widespread conviction among beekeepers that a relatively novel pesticide widely used to treat the seeds of biotech crops is causing the bees to lose their way home.

Certainly, 2009 began as another season of bee shortages in my garden; when the peach bloomed pink, the flowers flared unvisited, and below them the pendulous white flowers of the lowbush blueberries sat in quiet unmolested clusters. When I went over to talk to the local beekeeper to whom Alan and I had spoken years earlier, he agreed that pesticides and mites were still part of the problem.

"But you know what's really killing the bees, Joan?" he asked. "They're dying of unrequited love. They love what they do for us. We just don't love them back." What a theme for the whole planet! Our problem is that we don't love the earth's living workers—from microflora to megafauna, from pond scum to elephants—enough, although all of them are essential pieces of Nature's web. To take her free services for granted is to risk losing them; they'll be neither cheap nor easy to replace.

CHAPTER TWENTY

Asparagus

The only reasonable transition from bees to asparagus, I had planned to say, is that even if we lost the former we would still have the latter, since I was under the impression that bees did nothing for asparagus. But given the omnipresence of the World Wide Web, I thought I ought to check that. Asparagus has male and female plants and the female does flower and produce red berries, but I had assumed the wind took care of getting the flowers fertilized. And on a site called VegEdge, I was initially reassured—"Avoid spraying," it said, "when asparagus or crops in neighboring fields are flowering. Although bees do not pollinate asparagus, they sometimes visit the asparagus during bloom." Which I could have settled for, but alas, since I don't trust the Web, I kept browsing and found in chapter 6 of a book called *Insect Pollination of Cultivated Crop Plants* that "Wind is not a factor in asparagus pollination. Bees and primarily honey bees are responsible for the seed crop (Norton 1913, Jones and Robbins 1928, Jones and Rosa 1928)." Wow, look at those citation dates; scientists have known about the bees' involvement for a long time!

And this article provided experimental evidence.

Eckert (1956) caged one female and two male crowns to exclude all except tiny insects. He harvested only 6.2 g of seed, but an open plant near the cage produced 775 g of seed. He concluded that insect pollination was essential to commercial seed production and that growers should provide one to two colonies per acre to their seed fields for pollination purposes.

I put all this information up front, just to confirm what you have probably already discovered for yourself, that scientists are indomitable and inventive, and that the more facts the Web offers us, the more complicated is the truth.

What I think I know for sure about asparagus is that the most desirable plants are often all male, or what the catalogs call Supermale, and they are desirable because they use all their energy sending up those delectable shoots and none of it producing young. This preference for maleness in the species seems to make it even more embarrassing that my first conscious recognition of the vegetable's sexiness was when an environmental group I worked with printed up a bumper sticker showing bulky asparagus shoots just emerging from the ground beside the slogan KEEP IT UP WITH ORGANIC. Admitting such belated enlightenment would be embarrassing—I must have been over sixty at the time—if I were not a grower for whom asparagus evokes entirely other associations. For many years, asparagus has been tightly linked with frustration in my mind; only recently has it evoked something like delight.

Most people, I'm convinced, don't actually know what asparagus is or how it grows. At least visitors who walk my summer garden are inevitably confused when I respond to their curiosity about that clump of feathery ferns at one end of a raised bed by telling them it's "asparagus." "Where?" they ask, seeing nothing they would dream of eating, and I have to explain that they're looking at once edible asparagus stalks, long past their prime by now, that have morphed into the ferns they were meant to be. Asparagus is like that. After its eating season is past, it's easily mistaken for anything but. I heard a funny story recently about a skeptic visiting an organic farm. As he drove in, a field of four-foot-high asparagus ferns appeared off to the right. The skeptic turned to his host and said, "Well, that certainly proves your point about organic! Look at that dill!"

Field identification is further complicated by the fact that asparagus is the only *shoot* very many of us eat. We eat lots of roots and leaves and fruits, and even buds—artichokes, broccoli, brussels sprouts, and the like. But other than asparagus, there are only a couple of shoots—pokeweed and the sprouts of the fiddlehead fern—that are foraged in country places and consumed as human food. Until very recently they were very seldom found in markets, but now that some of us omnivores have become obsessed with novelty, almost everything edible is found in some produce bin.

The thing that makes a shoot different is just that. It's shooting—almost always up and early in the year—on its way to becoming something else. If you don't stop it on the way, you might as well forget it. Most vegetables do not have a long life span, but most of them don't metamorphose so dramatically so fast. Green beans hang on getting bigger and tougher, tomatoes get overripe and may even fall from the vine, but they still look like old beans and rotten tomatoes. Plants that bear beans and tomatoes can be viewed as having tomatoes and beans as their deeper purpose. But harvesting asparagus thwarts a plant rushing to make a woody, unchewable asparagus fern.

Another unusual thing about asparagus as a seasonal vegetable is that it comes up every year without being replanted. Unlike most vegetable crops, it isn't moved around to different parts of the garden in successive years: it's a perennial that loathes being transplanted. This means that when you grow asparagus, you have to think far ahead—a trait not widely encouraged in our society—to make sure you locate it in a part of the garden that you won't want to dig up in successive years. This requires rootedness on the part of the gardener—you can't move—and a level of advance planning that's not rewarded in much of life.

You may think you want to set the asparagus out where it can look glamorous in midsummer as a feathery asparagus fern border, but in a couple of years things may not work out that way and you may regret your initial decision. You can, of course, always try moving it to where you'd like it to be now; all I can say about that is "good luck." In my case, the several summer clumps of asparagus fern scattered around my small garden were until very recently remnants of beds that failed. But more about that later.

Growing asparagus from seed as one grows other garden plants is a long-term proposition, because its first sprouts look like . . . well, like little sprigs of dill. It can take three or more years for a plant to produce anything like a "bunch of asparagus," and even then the spears are mostly too slender to be interesting. However, my asparagus problems to date have nothing to do with its extended youth, but with the sheer physical difficulty of planting it properly when you don't start from seed, and with its apparent distaste for all the situations in which I've tried to grow it.

Asparagus is usually planted as "crowns" (two- or three-year-old roots) that any home gardener can buy from a mail-order house or a local garden center. I've planted a lot of these over the years, but my ability to produce enough asparagus to make it all worthwhile has been challenged every time I've tried it.

To begin with, the standard instructions for planting asparagus are fairly daunting. Here's one. After the usual warnings about choosing the site carefully, keeping the bed far enough away from other plants so they won't compete with it, and getting rid of *all* perennial weeds ("You won't get another chance to till the soil and destroy weeds for 15 to 20 years," the author sternly warns) the preparation begins:

> Dig a trench 12 inches wide and 15 inches deep and set the topsoil to one side. Add 4 inches of rich organic matter, preferably aged manure (compost or peat moss will do), then toss on about 2 inches of the topsoil and mix together in the bottom of the trench. Spread superphosphate fertilizer or bone meal to provide phospho-

rus—the key ingredient for strong root systems—at the
rate of 5 pounds per 100 square feet. Add another inch
or so of topsoil and mix it all together again. The planting bed should now be 6 inches or more below ground
level with plenty of topsoil waiting on the sidelines.[22]

I don't know how many of you readers have tried to empty
a deep trench—and in my case we're talking about a trench
three feet wide and fifteen feet long edged by a path of pavers on
either side—in a relatively small yard, but let me warn you that
it presents problems in terms of storing all that "topsoil" you're
setting to one side. Moreover when you get below the top six to
eight inches, not everything you're taking out is topsoil. Some of
it is subsoil—which, presumably, one needs to find someplace to
store separately.

So I've dug out the soil, separated it into the topsoil (piled
up on plastic sheets on the paths on either side of the bed) and
the not-so-topsoil (banished elsewhere), then I've put into my
fifteen- or eighteen-inch-deep trench four inches (roughly) of
aged manure or whatever, mixed in the superphosphate and
about half the topsoil, and, as instructed, I've made a mound
down the middle of my trench and I'm ready to plant. The worst
is yet to come.

What I'm planting are two-year-old asparagus roots. One
of my garden books describes them as looking like octopus or
squid. Mine don't look like that at all, whether I've bought them
from a mail-order house or from a local garden center. The fact
is they look a bit like cooked, crumpled, and redried whole wheat
ziti growing out in all directions from a center stem. Maybe if you
went to an asparagus field and dug up your own roots they would
have an orderly, vigorous appearance. Mine never do. They've
been crumpled together in a plastic pouch for a while, and they
look as dead as that squid would if she'd been treated that way.
It's hard to tell which roots are actually broken—and should be

cut off—and which are just bent, even after I've soaked them in a pail of water as instructed.

"The crowns should be centered right over the mound's crest, with their roots flowing downward over the mound's flanks." Well, I'm here to tell you that my roots never *flow*, downward or any other direction. I press them into place on the flanks of the mound that sinks under the pressure and cover them with dirt as instructed. When the whole dozen or two dozen plants have been treated this way, I cover the whole thing with about two inches of topsoil. I am instructed to mix the rest of the topsoil with manure or compost, leave it on the path, and gradually fill in the trench as the little ones grow. If they grow. The last time I tried this, I got only half the bed dug, in which I planted ten of the crowns. I wasted the other fifteen out of sheer exhaustion. Five of the ten grew, three survived their first winter, two survived their first spring, and so on. What I've just described was actually my second Piermont attempt at asparagus farming—an account of the first follows shortly.

Given the difficulties of growing asparagus, the fact that any of it turns up in the market for sale proves that there are talented farmers who are a lot better at this than I am. But they, of course, are up against the global market, so their association with asparagus may turn out to be as stress-filled as mine—though for other reasons. China produces prodigious quantities of white asparagus, largely canned, but we eat more green and Peru is growing that; competition from imports has reduced asparagus production in California, though I must insist that asparagus, this fresh and wonderful shoot, loses to travel much of what makes it worth eating.

My own history with asparagus goes back some years. When my husband was alive and we were living in the old Victorian we inhabited for thirty-six years, he and I planted asparagus, but we had so much trouble with competing tree roots that I don't recall ever harvesting anything to serve for dinner. So when we moved to our home on the west bank of the Hudson River, where there was lots of sun and no competing trees, we decided to do it right. We had already learned that our land was low, and that it flooded from time to time. We suspected that it would be a good idea to plant the asparagus high.

So when the building we had planned to renovate proved unsalvageable and had to be demolished, we reclaimed what parts of it we could, most notably lots of twenty-five-foot-long four-by-eleven-inch floor joists. Our plan to use them as exposed beams in the living room fell through—like most of our plans for the old house—but we saved them anyway and nailed some of them together to make—on either side of our five-foot-wide center path—two giant boxes fifteen feet long and three feet wide that would hold our asparagus above the anticipated floods.

My idea was to create a visual border between the fruit trees closer to the house and the vegetable beds running out to the river as well as to honor the asparagus plants' need for dry—or at least not sopping wet—feet. I pictured a dense border of asparagus ferns about which each summer's visitors would exclaim, "How lovely!"

So my husband and I built the boxes—with difficulty since four-by-eleven beams are heavy even when they're cut to fifteen feet. Then, just as we were about to put them in place, God sent us a warning. The morning of the nineteenth of March, we woke up to a yard filled with eighteen inches of water plus all the floating trash the river carried in—including what seemed an endless collection of pop-it plastic beads. We had been visited by a nor'easter. We cleaned up, the yard began to dry out, and we set the beam-boxes in place. Two weeks later, I called the mail-order nursery and learned that our order (which included fruit trees, raspberry canes, and rhubarb in addition to asparagus) had gone downstairs to shipping.

Planning to provide the asparagus with an ideal life, we filled the boxes with rich town compost mixed with some dirt and the requisite dose of phosphorus. Then we waited for our mail-order plants to arrive. The order arrived—into a yard drowned once more, this time because of torrential rains. No less daunting was the fact that on the morning we planted it was cold enough to form ice on the tops of the buckets in which we soaked the dry asparagus crowns. But gardeners persist.

So with frozen hands, we set each asparagus crown, like the heroine in the Princess and the Pea, onto its pillowy bed that sat ten inches above the wet yard. The roots did not flow down from the soaking-wet mound of earthy compost we had created for them, but we did our best. We set them a foot apart as ordered, and since we had two fifteen-foot beds and more than twenty-five plants (nurseries provide bakers' dozens where asparagus roots are concerned), we ended up with a few spares that I stuck out on the high and weather-beaten riverbank in soil so dead I had to whack it open with a hatchet. I knew it was pointless, but it seemed better than just throwing the crowns away.

The asparagus spears came up, slender but encouraging. We ate a few spears, watched the rest go to fern, and worked on other things in the garden. And then came fall. I had assumed the March flood was *it* for the year.

OCTOBER 19 . . . on October 18, the lord of the rivers chastised me for saying I didn't get enough exercise in fall. The river came to visit, once again more forcibly than it had visited before, and once again we had a yard full of Hudson river, old telephone poles, giant planks, sheets of plywood, plastic stuff (I hate plastic), and heaps of organic matter . . . Everything floated—the cold frame, all the buckets of fertilizer in the shed (whose floor is 18 inches above the low point in the yard), and the giant "boxes" containing the asparagus.

And so it was that the mighty Hudson, surging under the great wooden boxes it took three people to move into place, simply floated them inland so that they no longer embraced the asparagus bed, but snuggled up next to it, exposing the mounds of delicious compost and the roots it had covered to the river that filled the yard. The boxes were restrained from further travel by the heavy posts that framed the raspberry bed, but much of the compost into which we had tucked the squiddy little roots was washed away. What was left was sodden.

With the help of volunteer neighbors, we cleaned up once more, reset the "boxes" around the asparagus, filled in the missing compost around the edges, and spoke kindly to the young crowns. But they knew now what they were in for, and refused to flourish. For a couple of years we had a small serving of asparagus for one or two dinners. But the plants were clearly unhappy. In case I had doubts about water being the problem, the asparagus planted on the riverbank, without any soil preparation, sent up some giant spears for a couple of years after it was planted, in gratitude, I think, for not having its feet in water, but the poor soil eventually did it in, and very shortly it disappeared. So did most of the asparagus in the giant boxes. That was our first Piermont attempt—unsuccessful.

A few years ago, in the process of rethinking a lot of things, I rethought my first two asparagus escapades. I should probably mention here that the second time I gave up, after all that serious digging, I had fifteen floods in the garden—a record by any standard—so all my plants needed to be especially determined in order to survive. Obviously the asparagus were not. But I was unwilling to give up. As you know by now, I had deeply dug the bed, put in compost—the whole thing. So I decided to plant seeds there.

Planting asparagus from seed does have certain advantages— like the fact that you can prepare the bed, put in the seeds, and let the plants find the level at which they wish to spread their roots. You don't ever have to lay a hand on those squid. So if you're young enough, and not too impatient, growing from seed may be just the ticket. As for me, I'm no longer young, but I'm getting more patient, so late in the spring when I found I had only two survivors in my second asparagus bed, I decided to start over there with seed.

I sowed the asparagus ovules over the mix of soil and sand I'd originally put together to help the asparagus bed drain. There was a lot of vegetable stuff buried in the bed too, and after I tossed the seed around, I topped it with compost. Hard seeds take a while to germinate, so I waited and watered patiently through a dry summer for the seedlings to come up. And waited, and waited. Not one appeared.

The following year, I planted soybeans in the back two-thirds of the bed. The soybeans flourished. And when I began to harvest them—cutting the plants at the base and carrying them away to strip off their beans—I suddenly noticed that huddled about their stems were a few tiny dill-like seedlings—that were not, on closer examination, dill. My seedling asparagus! So I carefully harvested the soybeans, and before winter closed in I carefully transplanted each of the seedlings to make a nicely spaced bed of tiny, tiny asparagus plants. I put a stick next to each baby so that when spring came I would have this bed of little asparagus, their roots at the level they themselves chose.

Not so fast. The garden flooded a couple of times over the winter, which washed that modest layer of mulch off the soil and sent the little sticks floating away. And a few freezes and thaws heaved all the little plants out of the soil so that all but two them disappeared by the time they should have been coming up. And of the two older plants at the front of the bed—leftover from that second attempt at planting crowns—one died. So that left me with one two-year-old plant and two one-year-old plants and a sense that this enterprise was doomed to failure by the fact that asparagus just didn't like the accommodations I had to offer.

And then I went to California for a board meeting of an organization that tends to flourish best in lovely settings, and in a Mendocino County vineyard I saw the most beautiful stand of asparagus I had ever seen, growing out of a tumbled mass of what I think was limestone. I know the gardener, and he's gifted beyond my wildest dreams, but I may actually exceed him in simple dumb determination. So I came home and, looking around, began to pile rocks on the empty back of my so-called asparagus bed with the intention of taking up my surviving asparagus plants and setting them among the rocks. That winter I watched the not-yet-raised bed pooled in water and realized I might have nothing to move.

And so, in January, I called in Dave, who had built my stone wall, and asked if he also built raised beds. He did. Taking advantage of an absurdly warm winter, he came and built them for me on the south side of the garden before the month was out. And as I stood and looked at them, I thought how nice it would be to pile up a mountain of stone and have asparagus in the middle bed, a kind of hedge breaking up the line of eleven beds. I could move in the three leftover plants to start with, and another that I have not mentioned that sits way back in the yard—the only remnant of that original planting in those giant floating boxes. Given the length of my beds, I would need only about ten plants, and one of the nurseries I order from offered three kinds of asparagus plants—medium, heavy, and giant, with a six-dollar difference between ten of the smallest and ten of the largest. Beating down my natural tendency to add patience to the cheapest, I spoke sharply to myself. "Joan, you're not going to live forever. For God's sake if you want to eat your own asparagus, get the *giant.*"

Meanwhile, charged by my excitement over this potential new rocky promontory on the flat landscape of my garden, I tried to ignore the fact that even as Dave was building his boxes, the land was being flooded three days in a row by record high tides. And once again I came in to write in my journal.

I'm astonished at my own level of hope and optimism, my own capacity for recovery from despair. And when I looked out as I was writing, Dave was out there with his helper—the helper anchoring the raised beds (so they don't float!), Dave—in hope of stopping the leakage from the river—finishing up the repaved area at the foot of the garden with its new wall.

And so, if Nature is willing, I hope that I might have, one day, short of my nineties, an actual bed of asparagus. Then again I might not.

Even if I do finally manage to produce some edible spears, however, you're not likely to get steamed asparagus if you come to eat here. That's because I learned years ago what has become my default way of cooking this rare vegetable. Lay the spears side by side on a cutting board and then, holding the knife flat on a sharp diagonal to the board, slice them into inch-long pieces. Sauté these for a minute or two in olive—or my new discovery, grape seed—oil, salting lightly as you remove them from the stove, and serve. Better than popcorn, and intensely green in taste and color.

If you're alert, you've probably assumed you now know why—in this era when everything flies to us from elsewhere in every season—there seems to be a more recognized season for asparagus than there is for most other vegetables. You might think the reason why there's a week or two in spring when everyone is saying to everyone else, "The asparagus is in," is that asparagus, being a shoot, shoots up only in spring. You're partially right, but it's a bit more complicated than that.

As this novice asparagus grower learned the hard way, asparagus will continue to send up shoots for some time through the growing season, producing a thickening clump of stalks. But if you cut the emerging shoots beyond some as-yet-to-me-indeterminable time, you will seriously weaken the plant for future production. Asparagus sends up those shoots for a reason, after all, to make ferns that can exploit the photosynthetic energy of the sun to keep itself growing, and like the rest of what Nature does, you'd better not assume for too long that what she's putting out is all there just for you.

IV

Growing Older

> As long as one has a garden, one has a future.
> As long as one has a future, one is alive.
> —Frances Hodgson Burnett,
> "In The Garden"

CHAPTER TWENTY-ONE

Spring

I used to wonder why I couldn't keep myself indoors in the spring. I would check out the garden at dawn, come in for breakfast, and settle down to work. Minutes later I would realize I needed to check out the garden again. I always told myself I had forgotten something, but I hadn't. I just wanted to see if anything new and wonderful had happened since my last visit.

One day I realized what made spring's unfolding so irresistible. It's not really the prettiest season. In the Northeast—if tourists are any indication—that distinction officially belongs to fall. And a summer vegetable garden offers much more to look at, and eat, than a spring one. But its loveliness does not alone explain the deep call of this season. Nor, I think, is it simply that winter is ending. Lots of people love winter, love snow, are sorry when it ends. And spring in many places brings mud and black-flies. No, I believe spring's seductiveness arises from the fact that it presents one of the few situations most of us encounter that gets *better* day after day after day without our active intervention.

Most of what we have to deal with we can't really affect: the weather, catastrophes around the globe, much of what our own government does—even the Internet where our contributions are as flyspecks on a surface the size of the biosphere. And most of the things we *can* affect are degraded by contact with our ordinary lives. Unless we intervene on behalf of cleanliness and order, our clothes are unavoidably soiled, our desks fall into chaos, our e-mails pile up, our living spaces get trashed. Children especially demand lots of energetic input and tidying up if they are to turn out satisfactorily.

But in spring, Nature grows more touchingly beautiful every

day without our doing anything—and whether or not we're there to watch. One year I invited a dear friend of Japanese extraction to come to our home in Congers and sit beneath our weeping cherry in April—to honor Japan's tradition of Nature-watching. But the tree put on its car-stopping four-day show year after year whether she was there or not.

There's a name now for the sort of lovingness one learns to feel for this yearly generosity. It's *biophilia,* love of life (meaning, *all* life). Some scientists think humans are instinctively biophilic. Perhaps. But if they are, such tender affection for Nature has been largely overwhelmed in most "modern" people by other sorts of affections. Television and other electronic devices—to which people now devote more hours a day than to anything else except sleeping and their jobs—seem especially well designed to drown out any signals other than their own. But I am—perhaps as a result of my California upbringing, certainly as a result of my long involvement with gardening—deeply tied to Nature.

Theoretically, at least, Nature can easily tolerate our indifference as she goes about her business, but it's becoming clear that she cannot tolerate our clumsy interference with her carefully balanced systems that keep things going. All those things we drown her out with would go to pieces if she didn't do her yearly organizing, collecting energy from the sun to hold all life together. Early in my study of nutrition and biochemistry, I was told repeatedly that "equilibrium is death," a statement I found overdramatic until I finally understood what it meant.

Since life is always using up energy, all living things must take in something that they can convert to energy in order to remain alive. Plants have the capacity to use light energy from the sun directly, to photosynthesize—literally "create from light"— solid matter from nothing but water, air, and a few minerals. Humans and other animals are plant-dependent—they depend on getting their energy secondhand from eating plants or one another. They live, as one observer put it, in a "green thralldom."

When a plant can no longer photosynthesize, it dies. When an animal can no longer utilize the energy captured by plants, it dies. Then smaller organisms, the decomposers, begin to break down the once living tissue of dead plants and animals to simple molecules to produce energy for their lives. These molecules are then taken up by organisms capable of using solar energy to start the building cycle again.

It was a short story of Shirley Jackson's about a woman fearfully sitting in a hotel window watching the small crumblings of New York's unceasing decay that first triggered my understanding that even the nonliving, solid things we make from stone and metal require a continual input of energy, often human energy, if they are not to degrade. Bridges must be painted, quarried stone crumbles, windows must be caulked, metal tools must be oiled. Stone (and concrete) and metal take a long time to break down but like most things humans used and cast aside a hundred years ago, they are degradable by other living things and *are* biodegraded, ultimately to dust.

When our species found fossil solar energy and learned to make from coal and oil "plastic" materials that would return to dust very slowly if at all, we ensured that our civilization's death would be marked almost permanently by toxic chemicals and plastics.[23] But even though our lust for permanence has eclipsed Nature's time, it has not overcome it. Growth and degradation still occur and spring, among its other virtues, is our most joyous reminder that life is cyclic.

Once, in the years when I was the busy chair of a university department, living—like too many Americans—without public transportation, I used to time my drives to and from Manhattan so that I could catch the morning and evening news shows on our public radio station. One early-April morning, on my way to the city, I was transfixed by hearing a poet speak of the declining number of springs he would be alive to appreciate. I was sixty-five at the time. My active mother, shoved into a wheelchair by a stroke just before her ninetieth birthday, lived to be ninety-four. I quickly calculated. I had twenty-nine springs left—perhaps. But since my mother surely didn't "enjoy" her last four springs, that left maybe twenty-five.

When you are very young, twenty-five springs may seem like an abundance. To me it seemed disturbingly few. One busy spring, you could be stuck indoors for the ever-longer days leading up to the summer solstice. And that would be it—only twenty-four more to go. The sun would have begun its decline southward into fall and winter. Nature would have moved on. To have learned that my life would end in twenty-five years wouldn't have shocked me at all. There were already events I eagerly anticipated not being alive for; indeed, things I would be happy to miss seemed then to be occurring at an accelerating rate.

So a declining number of years of life didn't bother me. But numbering springs was different. It put tangibility into those intervening years. Would I be down to fifteen springs before the pawpaw tree I planted as a seed finally began to bear? Could I afford to wait until fall to fill out that perennial border with divisions of my own white astilbe? Or should I buy several plants right away—on credit like a modern gardener—so I can enjoy a finished border longer?

Spring-counting hit me particularly hard the year I was seventy-five. As I have had to say much too often, my garden floods, but what I have not said is that as the water sinks in, it sinks in most slowly in the middle of the yard where a green clover path runs down to the river. So every winter the clover takes a hit, low spots dying out in a sodden surly manner so they need reseeding; it's usually May before the path recovers.

Except for one particularly miserable May. That May—the wettest, cloudiest May on record—the path didn't recover, and by mid-June it was still bare in spots. This was, of course, depressing, as was the fact that because so much water had been asked to soak down into my already soaked soil, vegetable beds could not be dug and crops could not be planted in a timely way. Moreover, it began to be obvious that my fall-planted garlic was rotting, several of my early-planted potato plants were turning brown and disappearing, and the really warm-weather seedlings like basil and eggplant were gasping for air in the saturated soil. I bitched a lot about this unseemly weather, explaining to anyone who would listen that I was more frustrated than non-gardeners because I couldn't do my major spring workout.

But what had really affected me so profoundly was that we had lost spring. It wasn't just that the crops were delayed or dying. If I had to, I could obviously buy vegetables like other people do. But that wasn't the point. The long and gentle days leading up to the summer solstice—the longest day of the year—were always my favorites. But that awful year they never came. I was never able to work from dawn until after sunset, experiencing the pleasure of exhaustion in making the garden produce both beauty and vegetables, and then going up to sit on my terrace to watch the sunset come over the shoulder of my house and reflect off the water while I ate whatever I had picked as I went about my garden chores.

I knew even then that we would have sunny days for sure. There is a historical record of only one year without summer in my vicinity. And much of the garden would surely recover— producing enough green beans, I hoped, to make me tired of them, and so many tomatoes that I would despair of getting them put up before they rotted. But spring was irrevocably gone. If I had fifteen springs left going into that year, I found myself by June down to fourteen. Which was not enough.

CHAPTER TWENTY-TWO

A Fate Worse than Death

There are lots of things to worry about as you grow older: how long you will be able to continue living where you now live, how long you will stay healthy, whether or not you should risk yoga despite your scoliosis, when you will die, and so on. After careful reflection, I believe that what I am most afraid of is falling into the hands of doctors before I pass on. My feelings about doctors have deep roots and are based almost entirely on experience.

Once many years ago, when I was passingly thought of as an expert on nutrition and development in pregnancy, I was asked to speak on that topic to a group of medical students at Yale, and to have lunch afterward in the dean's office with some of the faculty. I think I surprised the students with my informality—as a late bloomer in academia I had not managed to internalize academic demeanor.

Actually, the sleep-deprived students seemed less surprised than exhausted; the faculty, however, were wide awake. They were getting all excited about nutrition, about how they might put together a curriculum that would begin at the deepest level with cellular nutrition and proceed scientifically all the way out to the edges of the body where they would be able to conclude definitively what people should put in their mouths. I agreed that it was a wonderful idea, but cautioned that we knew far too little to do it.

While they could likely reach some pretty good biochemical conclusions about how cells were nourished, and while I or others could probably give them some pretty good ideas about what sorts of diets seemed historically consistent with good health and long life, they were going to run into a huge gap in the middle when they tried to tie together what they had learned about cellular nutrition with actual eating recommendations.

If you took iron as an example, it would prove dauntingly complex to make careful measurements of things like exactly how iron got utilized in the body if the consumer had an excess of iron already in storage. And quantitatively, what would be the effect of consuming an iron-containing food where the iron was bound by other substances in that food, or consuming it at a meal containing some vitamin C that would enhance absorption.

How could all those—and hundreds of other variables involving other biochemicals that just happened to be in the food along with the iron—be measured within some reasonable level of certainty? All those things were unknown, I said, and would probably remain unknown because when the thousands of biochemicals in food interacted, with one another and with the thousands of biochemicals in the human body, there were just too many variables to allow anyone to carry out neat experiments.

They weren't happy with what I said. And they were even unhappier afterward when I remarked enthusiastically that as I listened to them I had suddenly understood that in a large sense medicine *was* nutrition. We all knew, I said, that doctors couldn't make you well if the body didn't cooperate. Doctors could only intervene in an ongoing process in the hope that some drug they prescribed for you or some part they sewed together or cut out would allow the body to heal itself.

If it was the case—and it was, I said—that the body made itself better and medicine's intervention in the disease process could do little more than give the body a chance to catch up, so to speak, then what medicine should be working on was figuring out how to make the body fight back. Since nutrition was a discipline decidedly lower on the power chain than medicine, there was a sort of stunned silence before one of the physicians said, "I think we'd have a little trouble with the medical school faculty."

We live in a society addicted to technology and what is thought of as progress, and we have been encouraged, since childhood—especially since my childhood when there was polio and someone found a vaccine that allowed us to go to the movies in the summer or to go swimming again—to believe that one day "they" would solve it for us. There has even been a notion, repeatedly revived, that one day a pill would be concocted that would nourish us completely so we wouldn't have to bother cooking or even eating.

It has been a help in my own life that I was a fact-obsessed pre-medical student in college and that I learned early and hard that there were no antibiotics for viruses—which is most of what infect us; and that when you had a fever—or one of your children had a fever—there was really no point in calling a doctor unless it was frighteningly high because until there were other symptoms, the doctor wouldn't know what it was either. I must say that my stance caused no end of problems with my mother-in-law, who considered it recklessly dangerous that I failed to call a doctor when one of her grandsons fell sick. Yet both are alive and healthy today.

And I have excellent proof of the general notion that doctors often don't have answers in one of my adult efforts to "deal with" a body problem that has plagued me for years. Many years ago—probably more than a decade—I became aware that the last two toes on my left foot were slightly numb. I wasn't sure it mattered, but continued to notice the odd feeling.

I was not particularly alarmed because I knew that my long-time family physician, who had recently moved to Annapolis, had long suffered from a numb-foot problem himself. And being a physician and brilliant diagnostician, he had naturally paid immediate attention to it, thinking it might be a chemical toxicity related to compounds he had been exposed to in his practice. Unable to diagnose the problem himself, he had finally gone to the Mayo Clinic, which had assured him after a battery of tests that his discomfort was not life threatening and probably not a chemical reaction; but they had no idea what it was. Which only goes to show that doctors share our problems.

My own discomfort spread across my left foot and ultimately all the toes were slightly numb—not so I didn't know which one you were grabbing if I stuck my foot at you, but like they were coated with mud where they hit the floor. Flash slightly forward. It's now December 1997, seven months after Alan's death. Here's what I wrote in my journal:

> **DECEMBER 15** My feet have been bothering me, feeling numb, like I am coming out from having them asleep. Sometimes it bothers me hardly at all. Sometimes they really burn and feel lousy . . . But it continues, so I made a doctor's appointment.
>
> And today I found myself in the doctor's waiting room, and ultimately in his examining room and he came in in a jolly mood . . . He did my feet, did my blood pressure . . . and then he had me lie down and he began palpating around my middle and writing things down. I asked what he was writing and he said he would tell me later. When I sat up he said that there was a little extra pulse in my abdominal aorta and that he was worried about an aneurism! So he wanted me to go have a sonogram. Swell.

So, on the morning of my sonogram, I got up early and had a big breakfast before seven o'clock so I didn't have to go hungry the whole morning. Then I did what I could to work. Not one to fantasize the worst, I was not really uptight, figuring the doctor was living out his own concern about having "missed" Alan's cancer. Nevertheless, I was unsettled and not until I showered and dressed and was just going out the door did the reason hit me: It was December 17, exactly the day that, just one year earlier, Alan had had a sonogram. Two days later he learned he had cancer. This was spooky.

I went over to the imaging center, signed up, waited, was called into the examining room, and said to the technician, "I need to tell you that this is fairly traumatic for me. My husband came in for a sonogram exactly one year ago today and he's dead." She didn't bat an eyelash. She didn't even say she was sorry. I lay down, and she began running her little instrument over me, again and again, and I began to suspect she was going over it so much because she saw something. Finally she said, "How are you doing?" And I snapped back, "I think I ought to ask you that." She said, "So far I haven't seen anything." Pause. "But I haven't looked at the place he was worried about." Swell again.

When it was over, she said nothing and I didn't ask, assuming, naturally, that her silence meant she had seen something awful. So I came home, had lunch, and called the doctor's office. Then I tried to work. Several phone calls later, the office called. Everything was fine. Whew.

So I didn't have an aneurysm but I still had numb feet.

Two years later I tried a course of acupuncture with a woman in a nearby town. The big news in this case is not that it helped— it didn't—but that when the doctor read the intake form on which I had listed my complaints, she looked up and said, "Oh, you have that foot problem everyone has."

"Really?" I exclaimed delightedly. "Do lots of people have it?"

"Well," she answered, "it's probably just that I see a lot of it because I'm sort of the end of the line." A lovely modest answer and I would loved to have continued going to her office to lie quietly listening to music while the needles played around my body, but after six sessions there was no change—and the acupuncturist didn't know what to call my persistent problem either.

Flash forward to August 2003, six years after my foot problem surfaced. I have a new doctor, in the city, very smart, very simpatico. His wife and a friend run the office. They know your name when you come in. Except for the fact that his name is unpronounceable and unspellable, he's perfect. I've even had the guts in my old age to call this (relatively) young man by his first name. After all, I reason, if I ask my students who are even younger, to call me Joan, I'm entitled.

Meanwhile, my foot problem has spread to both feet and I figure it's time to try again. This *might* be something serious. So on my first appointment I say, "Stanley, I've got this foot problem . . . ," and I describe it. He grunts, continues with the exam, and when he finishes, I have prescriptions for blood pressure medication, an aortic Doppler and an echocardiogram, plus an abdominal sonogram searching for the same abdominal aneurism for which the last doctor had me take a sonogram. When I explained to him that I'd already had a sonogram for that, he said it could have happened since.

> **AUGUST 13** I have just made an appointment with Mid-Rockland Imaging—again—and before I hung up the woman who made the appointment said "feel better." And I laughed and said "I feel great. This is all the result of my going to a doctor . . ." And I added, "I was out moving sandbags yesterday so I must be OK." She laughed.

And so, continuing on my medical search, I ended up with a second abdominal sonogram, which again turned up negative. I didn't have an aneurysm, but I still had numb and sometimes swollen feet.

I waited awhile before trying again, but on one visit where Stanley and I were on particularly good terms because my blood pressure was way down, I made the pitch. "Okay, Stanley, I know you doctors don't know what on earth to do about my feet because two of you have given me abdominal sonograms to avoid talking about them. I don't want another sonogram, but do you know anything about what's wrong with my feet?"

His response was not precisely an answer, but he did say, "Well, Joan, there's a drug that seems to give some people relief." And I looked at him over my reading glasses and said, "Stanley, you know I'm not going to take a pill that just might help a bit. So nobody really knows what it is?" He changed the subject.

And so, convinced that I would just have to live with my numbing feet, I made no further medical plans until a friend who had pulled a tendon on a walking trip overseas was raving about the podiatrist she had just found. Aha! One more chance. It's my feet; maybe a podiatrist is the answer. And so I made an appointment with Renee Sliva.

It was the first of July when I drove up to Nyack—warm weather and my feet hurt—and discovered her office just riverward of the best pastry shop in the county. Now, that's placement. She was a delight, and told me all the right things—really knew what was going on and said my feet were in great shape! My nerves were being impinged on by the surrounding tissue, as happens when your feet have walked thousands of steps (she used an exact number, since she seemed to have in her head a number of steps per year to multiply by eighty!). She told me my feet were in great shape given my age and that she could tell the circulation was excellent because I had hair on my toes! I had never even thought of that as an asset.

I got a tuna sandwich next door, plus something gooey for dessert, and went home to celebrate. I still have numb and sometimes burning feet. But somebody who knows feet admires mine, and as long as I have hairy toes, I don't have to worry that I'm having trouble with my circulation. Even in the face of continuing discomfort, knowledge is power—and reassurance.

Knowledge and the Internet (which are not interchangeable entities). I bring up the Internet because the last time I approached the medical system, it was Google that allowed me to confirm my view of medical ignorance. There was nothing but nearsightedness wrong with my eyes when I went to get my vision tested. At least I had no noticeable complaints, as was confirmed by consistently checked "nos" on the sheet listing possible eye problems that I filled out at the ophthalmologist's office where I had made an appointment for a routine vision test.

This was an office I'd never been to before, and I was there not because I was unhappy with the eye doctor I had previously used but because he was across the county and all I needed was a vision test ("can you read this line without glasses?") in order to renew my driver's license. I figured I could find a place closer to home to have the test.

A 'Net-savvy friend went online, punched in something, and there on my screen was a map with every site within several miles tagged, including a place in nearby Orangeburg. Terrific. I called, confirmed that I could have a vision test without buying anything (I assumed that the vision centers at the county's two malls wouldn't give you a test unless you were buying glasses), and made an appointment.

I got a confirming call before I went, and on the appointed day I went to have my vision test. As I went in, I became aware that the office had a large area where they sold glasses, and sat down to await my call. I was called, went into an examining room, and was told by a young woman to look into some eyepieces on one apparatus and to stare at the red dot on another. I did so, after which I was asked to stare into some other apparatus to report something else. Then I was left alone for a few minutes, after which a different young woman asked me to read some type (now we're getting somewhere) and was told the doctor would see me shortly.

In a few minutes a man came in, looked closely into my eyes with some sort of scope, muttered something, pulled away, and said: "You have cataracts."

"I know," I said. "The doctor I normally go to told me six years ago that I had them, but about three years ago when I went back, he didn't mention the cataracts. When I asked about them, the doctor said they hadn't progressed at all."

"Oh," said today's doctor, "it isn't a matter of whether they've progressed, but whether they interfere with your vision. And it's only about a ten-minute operation.

"Here," he added, holding a card first over my left eye and then over my right, "notice that your right eye is worse than your left one."

"Yes, I see that it's a little less clear, but it doesn't bother me."

I was puzzled that he seemed to be encouraging me to have a cataract operation since I remembered from the experience of my mother and others who'd had it that the doctor usually waited until a cataract had really "developed" and was "ripe" before it was removed—so that one eye was normally done before the other while the second one ripened.

I discovered why he was so enthusiastic, of course, when I came home after the visit and looked up the cost of cataract surgery on the Web. I discovered that ordinary cataract surgery was covered by Medicare and that it would cost an estimated $3,363 per eye. Since my operation would be covered by Medicare, why wouldn't I just go ahead and have my lenses removed? Is it any wonder we see our health care costs rising wildly?

Since I seemed not to want to have my undeveloped cataract removed, the doctor moved on. "The glands at the base of your eyelashes are plugged," he continued. "They are not allowing lubrication to flow so your eyes are dry." Dry eyes was a condition I had *not* checked on the form I filled out, nor, even more important perhaps, had I noticed it on a day-to-day basis. My eyes don't seem dry, don't itch, and simply don't bother me, even though I sometimes overuse them. But who am I to know whether my formerly unacknowledged eyelash glands are plugged?

Without asking me whether my "dry" eyes bothered me, he handed me two samples, and then wrote up prescriptions for the two drugs being sampled. He then instructed me to use one four times a day for a month and the other every night before bed. After which I was shown the door and told to make an appointment to come back in a month. His minions did sign my Department of Motor Vehicles form allowing me to continue to drive without glasses.

As I stood at the desk, waiting for the prescription to be completed, I was handed a form that would give me twenty dollars off on one of the drugs. Twenty dollars off *what*, I wondered. What was the price for a month? What *were* these drugs? I took the samples, the prescriptions, and what was left of my good humor and went home without having the prescriptions filled. I didn't open the samples, and that night I went to bed unmedicated.

The next day, I opened the sample of the twenty-dollar-off drug and took out the double-sided insert printed in type so small I needed a magnifying glass to read it. I got a magnifying glass and read it. It was amazing. Among the first things I read was, "If the symptoms do not abate in two days, see your doctor." What symptoms? How would I know if they had abated since I didn't have any?

The next thing it said was "Do not continue use more than 28 days," and it went on to list possible side effects that included glaucoma. So this licensed eye doctor—a supposed specialist who knew nothing whatsoever about my general health or mental state—I'm over eighty after all and could be senile—had given me a drug to use for a month that was capable of causing serious side effects if misused.

But because I'm loath to throw anything away, I opened the sample bottle and tried to put a drop in each eye. After several misses that hit my cheek, I managed it. My eyes bothered me all day. I'm sure by the time I went back a month later, I would have really needed help. So I threw away the instructions, the samples and the prescriptions and a week later (I had to let a decent time elapse of course to be courteous) I cancelled my appointment.

But before I did, I couldn't resist going on the Web and

Googling "clogged eyelid glands." Sure enough, there was a site called—aptly enough—

> clogged eyelid oil glands—Information, Symptoms, Treatments and Resources

on which the first post was August 24, 2008:

> Good Morning, Yesterday I was diagnosed with cataracts & clogged eyelid oil glands.

Woo-hoo. She must have gone to the same doctor I did! I didn't look further for whatever advice the Web had to give.

Based on all of the above, my best health advice would have to be to stay away from doctors unless absolutely necessary. And in the final analysis, I say this not only because—as I tried to tell the doctors at Yale—your body is what will make you well or not, and not only because of my foot and eye experiences, but because learning from doctors about problems neither you nor they can do anything about is as likely to ruin your remaining life as anything else you can think of. I want to end my medical saga with an example of this that is, I hasten to admit, pretty trivial.

As you probably know, most people, perhaps the majority of people my age and even much younger, are found to have one or more slipped disks if examined by X-ray or other techniques for looking inside the body. Yet most people do not have pain from this condition, and many people who have back pain and have their "slipped disks" repaired do not resolve their back pain. Spinal explorations are tricky.

A couple of years ago, I got what was probably *Giardia*—a nasty little organism that multiplies in the gut and is hard to diagnose. (I know *Giardia* better than most people might because I took bacteriology as a pre-med and I have a vivid picture of this tear-shaped object with a large eye-spot and clusters of fishhooks hanging off its body.) Although the medical profession in this case managed to extend my period of illness amazingly, due to lost records, failure to test for *Giardia* when my stool was tested (at my request), and the like, eventually I was cured by a doctor who said, "Oh well, since they failed to test you and you've been waiting this long, I'm going to treat you as if you have *Giardia*"— and he finally cured me.

But long before that, when a friend decided I had spent too many weeks feeling miserable, she insisted that I go see "someone." She accompanied me to one of those walk-in clinics where I had gone once before to be treated for stepping on a nail. Listening to me complain about my gut, the doctor decided he wanted a look-see and ordered an X-ray. I am more X-ray-averse than I am doctor-averse, but I was in no condition to protest. So I let them zap me, and pretty soon the doctor came over and, pointing to the X-rays he had clipped to the wall, said with real gusto, "You have very bad scoliosis. Look at all that degeneration there." I was seventy-four at the time. I had lived my whole life without ever knowing I had scoliosis—which I now understand I was probably born with—and I really didn't want to know.

But there it was, that S-curve of the spine—I was seriously damaged! Now, as a gardener, I do major digging every year and repeated hauling of bags of manure, sand, compost, and the like, and I almost never have back problems. But for at least a year after I saw that awful picture, every time I got a crick in my back, I thought, "Oh my, my whole spine could go anytime. One day I won't be able to get out of bed," and so on.

Fortunately, I have a dancer friend to whom I said one day, "You know, I've been having these pains which I assume are caused by my scoliosis and I also assume that there's not much I can do about them."

"I think you're right about the first," she said, "but not about the second." She sent me to a good physiatrist she knew, I was given some stretching exercises, and after a week I had no pain. And when a pain does come back—since of course I don't do the exercises regularly—I stretch for a couple of days and it's gone. But I sure wish I had never seen that picture.

None of this is meant to say doctors don't know anything. They are just able to help us much less than we have been led to believe, and since they want to help—and avoid getting sued— they do to you what they know how to do, even if it makes your quality of life worse as you age and die. So as I think about my rapidly approaching old, old age, getting trapped in the medical system is almost the only thing I really fear.

CHAPTER TWENTY-THREE

Kicking My Tires

On the first day after my eightieth birthday, but a week before a big potluck friends were giving to celebrate my entry into my ninth decade, I found myself trying to decide how I felt. Because that's what everyone asked me. "What does it feel like to be eighty?" Of course the question is mostly social, something to begin the conversation. Everyone knows that being eighty doesn't feel significantly different from being seventy-nine, which is what I was a few hours earlier, or seventy-eight, which I was a day and a year before this birthday. My interlocutors certainly don't want me to launch into an introspective catalog of my thoughts in the hours since I turned four score. What they really mean by the question, I think, is "How *are* you? Feeling okay, lonely, running down?"

This apparent curiosity about how you are starts well before eighty. I don't know exactly when but it's sometime after you "retire," as I recall, that people begin asking with a very particular intonation, "And how *are* you," with the accent on the *are*, right after they say "Hello, Joan"—as if they're braced to hear the worst. Perhaps the operative assumption is that you want permission to give what a dear old friend of mine once described as "an organ recital." "Well my eyes are okay, my lungs still work, and my stomach's fine, but I've lost some hearing and I really notice my bladder."

Aging is a funny thing. I'm pleased to finally be eighty. The ages leading up to it seem so elderly. There's something that feels complete about eighty; it's not "almost eighty," or "coming up on eighty," or any of the other ruses I've used to avoid the pedestrian seventy-seven or seventy-eight or seventy-nine. I'm happy to be eighty—especially considering that the alternative is not to be here at all—but I'm not sure I'm happy about how people think of me when they hear my age or, even worse, look at me and judge me to be officially old.

I vividly remember the first time a woman whom I would have assumed to be old offered me her seat in the subway—a woman! I've almost never been offered a subway seat by a man, even when, loaded with a heavy backpack and looking as old as I can manage, I stand right in front of one of those large-thighed young men who sit splay-legged so as to occupy at least two and a half subway seats. It's always women who either get up, or catch your eye and give a little nod to indicate *you* should sit down. The thing is, when women offer you a seat you know it's not because you're a woman, but because they assume you're older and feebler than they are.

How you really are, of course, when you're my age has a lot to do with whether you inherited good genes and whether you've taken some care of their expression as you've lived your life. I suspect my genes are pretty good—at least half of them, since my mom lived to be ninety-four—let me amend that, she survived to ninety-four. She lived until ninety when a big stroke put her in a nursing facility to which, as she consistently made clear, she would have preferred the alternative—in her case, heaven. And my father's life, all sixty-eight years of it, was foreshortened, I'm certain, by the fact that he lived with so much repressed anger that came out mostly as allergies, headaches, backaches, and the like. But he had a chubby older brother who lived well into his nineties so I suspect his family's *genes* were good.

As for having taken care of my genetic endowment, I used my body constantly as a young Southern Californian living where outdoor play happened year-round. And where my diet is concerned, I'm sure my mom tried; I certainly *had* to eat vegetables. But her idea of salad—a slice of iceberg lettuce dressed with lemon juice and sugar, for her daughter who didn't like her

"French dressing" made with catsup—was sufficiently off-putting that I still don't put salad in the "must-have" category.

And except for canned spinach, I can't think of a vegetable I really enjoyed during those California years when I could have had anything fresh. Looking back, I find the canned spinach deviation astonishing; I haven't touched it since I left home, but the fact that Popeye ate it may have affected me more than I dare acknowledge. I did eat a lot of fruit. Oranges were abundant and cheap; seasonal fruit was always there. But even though we had an avocado tree in our California backyard, I didn't learn to like avocados until I came to New York. And during my years as a single woman at *Time,* I had a generally rotten diet, often a Coke and a chocolate bar from the vending machines for breakfast.

But in reflecting on my adult diet—that is, what I ate after I married, had children, and studied nutrition—I suspect it earned me some health credits. While pregnant, thanks to my brother-in-law, I read health-food guru Adele Davis who was heavy into vitamins and protein, and fatty, vitamin/protein-rich liverwurst long before animal livers were thought of only as the last resting place of industrial toxins. So I ate a lot of liverwurst and gained weight, and I tried hard to put healthy food on the table. Then as I aged my life moved strongly into food production, and eating what I grow, so my diet has probably undergone constant improvement in the last twenty years.

I was spending some time recently thinking a bit more about bees and their mysterious disappearance, and wondering whether the bees aren't dying of malnutrition; they are moved around to orchards and live on really restricted diets, nothing but almond nectar, for example, for long periods of time. Their self-chosen diets would have a variety of nectars, including some from protective wild herbs. And that led me to wonder whether the very instability of my present eating environment might be helping me stay so healthy in old age. I'm not "working out," as I have earlier reported, and I confess I am eating out more than is probably good for me, although some of my restaurant food is locally produced, and hence largely seasonal.

But when I eat at home, I have to keep shifting what I eat to keep up with what the climate is doing to my crops. So it may be that a bad year for production is part of what keeps me vital. The potatoes did well this year—not perfectly but fine enough that I can count on them—the sweet potatoes gave promise of a good crop even before I finished digging them, and the carrots and beets are flourishing, which means I'll have them available for much of the winter in my hydrator drawer and elsewhere.

But the tomatoes were hit hard by blight and failed to recover in the cooler fall weather as they usually do, which means I have put away less tomato sauce and puree than I normally make. And harlequin beetles hit the brussels sprouts so I'm not going to have many, if any, of them for January. The peppers did so well that I've had to learn how to use more of them to supplement tomatoes; the Tuscan kale that I grew for the first time ultimately survived the beetles that did in the brussels sprouts; and so on. As one of the articles I was reading this week says, "Redundancy ensures reliability, so if one component of the system fails, there is always another able to replace it."

And although my choices seem narrower than those of people whose food is selected from the thirty thousand *odd* (a deliberately chosen modifier!) products in the supermarket, the plight of the bees on their modern diet reminds me of the underlying narrowness of our modern diet in which corn, soy, and sugar feature heavily in the great majority of those food-like items on the grocery shelves. It's possible that our current health catastrophe—the frightening statistics on obesity and diabetes among other things—may be the human version of Colony Collapse Disorder, from which my garden protects me.

Moreover, I've finally realized that the "How *are* you?" question my friends ask is the verbal equivalent of kicking the tires of a car you're wondering if you should buy. Both approaches are ineffectual at figuring out whether the kickee can still go—which I can. But the question really means "*What* are you? Are you interesting enough to talk to—even though you're old?" To which I would like to reply, if only it were asked directly, "Well, I think I am, but you'll just have to find out for yourself." What I do instead is answer the question they actually ask. "Oh I'm fine," I say brightly, skip the organ recital, and launch off into politics or world affairs—or the garden. I have no idea how to behave differently until I feel different, and—except for a bit more reluctance to go out and work when the weather isn't good—I don't.

Actually, now that you ask, I'm fine. I do have scoliosis. And I don't want that to get so bad that I can't stride down the street for the next ten years or so on my funny feet, but it doesn't hurt, and it's certainly not the main thing on my mind. Well, sometimes it is. I was talking to another aging friend of mine once about how much better I looked in the mirror first thing in the morning when my back was relatively straight and my belly reasonably flat, than at the end of the day when everything seemed to have collapsed into bulges in reaction to a day of uprightness. She laughed and said, "Yeah, that gravity—it's awful."

CHAPTER TWENTY-FOUR

Losing It

I guess you could say I'm "losing it," except that what is usually meant by that phrase is not at all what seems to be happening to me. I remember things, often things that have no apparent purpose for me, like Wirsung's duct (pronounced *Virsung's*), the name of the secondary duct of the pancreas, something I learned with no particular emphasis almost sixty years ago when I was a pre-medical student and have never been able to forget. But I am also pretty good at remembering where I left my coffee cup, when I last used my keys, what I went out in the garden to do this morning, and so on, and I can still get up in front of a group of people and speak coherently—even finding my way back from diversions, most of the time. In other words, I don't think that in the jargon of the day I'm "losing it."

But in quite another sense I am. The latest manifestation of this loss came to me the other morning as I was reading about the concern of the citizens of Boston over possibly losing their major newspaper. It was but one of a spate of truly alarming stories about how quite abruptly, with what seems like very little warning, our newspapers—those packages that use to land with a thud on our sidewalks or front porches every morning no matter where we lived—are disappearing.

Environmentally, I have very mixed feelings about this, of course; I've suffered guilt for years about the forests that are cut down to provide me with what must by now be thousands of pounds of newsprint, a huge percentage of which I never manage to read. I do recycle it all—a habit I got into during World War II—but that doesn't make up for the waste. I don't even look at the ads, so I'm not helping the paper by patronizing its advertisers. Truth to tell, given the information overload of the Web, I only continue to subscribe to the *Times* to encourage them to keep printing the paper.

But what I realized suddenly as I read about the failure of *The Boston Globe* was that in future years, there would be no need for one of the skills I used to be really proud of: how to identify any one of the more than a hundred papers stacked on the shelves of the "clip desk" at *Time* magazine just by the look of their headlines and body type as it showed on their folded edges. I used to take pride in being able to pull out a copy of the *Seattle Post Intelligencer*—now dead in printed form after 146 years—with just a quick glance at the shelves on which the newspapers were stacked. And that example is merely symbolic. As I see it, the problem isn't losing one's useful skills as one ages; it's that the skills one possesses are rendered as useless by the passage of time as was the proverbial buggy whip.

Theoretically there are other skills one might acquire, to fill the empty places so to speak, except that the new skills that seem to be taking over the world—blogging, texting, Twittering, Facebooking—don't really seem worth my time, despite the assurances of some of my young friends that they are. I did actually try Facebooking for a week or two, and I had one experience with producing a story that got "into"—no, I don't think that word applies anymore—it got "onto" The Huffington Post. I was told it was going to be there, and when it "went up," I went to The Huffington Post and looked for it. It may have been there for twenty minutes or so between 10 and 11 PM, but after that you would have had to search for my name—which is what I did to see it—to know it had ever appeared. You wouldn't just come across it glancing through the paper. There's something so profoundly evanescent about such an accomplishment that it's hard to know why anyone would want to attempt it.

I find myself reminded of a Lewis Thomas quotation I read once:

This why it is so hard being a juvenile species, still milling around in groups trying to construct a civilization that will last. Being useful is easy for an ant.[24]

Which is a comforting idea to reflect on, I think, as one gets far enough along in life to wonder what old age is good for! Because Lewis Thomas's assumption of ant self-satisfaction assumes that since all humans are members of a juvenile species, doubt about what it means to be useful is not limited to the elderly.

Before I formally left the salaried workforce, I remember that getting a check provided me with an assurance of usefulness that must be something like being part of an ant colony. It's not that troubling questions about living never arose. It's just that when you regularly encountered middle-of-the-night doubts, you could assure yourself that if what you were doing was not useful, *they* would not be paying you to do it. Someone better paid than you had decided your "work" activity was worth money—useful at least for helping your employer succeed at whatever she was trying to accomplish.

Which is, I'm sure, one of the reasons why losing one's job is such a painful experience; in this "advanced" society, we're not encouraged to define our usefulness in more human ways—indeed, our usefulness to those who spend the most time trying to influence us is based pretty thoroughly on our ability to consume. We are useful to the economy because we buy; so losing a job means we lose both identity and purchasing power simultaneously.

In my post-retirement years, I find some reassurance in the fact that I am still paid, for four months in the fall, for professing a course I have now taught for more than a third of a century. But once that's over at the end of each December, I have to assure myself of my usefulness without remuneration.

Others feel the same, I know. I had an e-mail from a post-eighty-year-old friend the other day that began,

> I managed to send a picture by e-mail when [my son] was here, but I have completely forgotten the art now. It is very perplexing to be old. Nothing much good lies ahead.

I'm really not quite that gloomy about life in general. I think some good things lie ahead, even in my old age—especially if Nature will lay off these waves of thunderstorms she keeps sending through. But I confess that I have limited expectations from a culture whose memory for the lessons of the past and whose grasp of the challenges to come are being shaped by media that measure their success in minutes, asking of their users little more than idle curiosity and rage toward either the right or the left. And since I don't trust people trained like that to take care of the planet, I'm glad that one of my skills that hasn't lost its usefulness is knowing how to grow food.

But given the possibility I may one day get too creaky to plant my own, I'm thrilled—and reassured—by how many young people seem to be opting out of a life spent entirely in cyberspace—however up to date that keeps them—and looking for a life in touch with the land; whatever happens to industrial agriculture when the world runs short of cheap oil, it looks like there will be young farmers out there to help keep us fed.

But there's more to my sense of continuing relevance than that. It looks as if all sorts of skills that I have honed despite a go-go culture telling me they're a waste of time may turn out to be widely useful after all. For it is not only young people who are suddenly interested in engaging with the land; suburban homeowners for whom a weedless lawn was the previous pinnacle of gardening achievement are digging up turf and turning it over to broccoli and tomatoes, and some of them are even asking for my advice. (Actually, if they ask for my advice in time, I tell them not to dig it up, but to mulch it down with newspapers or cardboard and plant right through the turf.)

Even nonconsuming is coming back; though initially driven to not-buying by economic stress, we are moving into a time when reusing plastic bags as I have done for years no longer marks one as cheap or pathologically conservationist. And my ability to compost and recycle so diligently that I can't even fill the small trash container under my sink in two weeks now seems a skill worth emulating. As we wind down from our two-hundred-year petroleum-fueled party, I find myself looking forward eagerly to my nineties when it will matter less that I don't Twitter than that I remember how not to waste.

CHAPTER TWENTY-FIVE

When I Am Ninety-Six

When I am ninety-six I hope I am not spending my early-spring mornings, as I spent the second beautiful dawn of this reluctant April, cleaning up plastic crap floated in by the Hudson. Arriving with the ruin when the river, pulled by a massive nor'easter, decides to flood my yard is the wrack—not only driftwood of all shapes and sizes, but some of the less appealing and ultimately, alas, more permanent remnants of our throwaway society. This morning's catch—to use an undeservedly sprightly word for the blue, green, white, black, and only occasionally red "things" I picked up—included the following:

- Twenty-odd plastic-bag remnants of various sizes and a small dirty brown plastic bag in which they now rest for disposal.
- Thirteen screw-on bottle caps, two push-on bottle caps, three of the little ruffled rings left on the neck of a bottle when you take the cap off, one lid for a foam plastic cup.
- Five of those little foam S's used for packing and thirty-three indefinable pieces of plastic foam, exclusively blue and white, many of which seem to come from foam coffee cups.
- Ten beat-up pieces of *hard* plastic, all blue and white.
- Four remnants of plastic soda straws.
- Three disposable cigarette lighters.
- Two badly mangled tampon inserters.
- One foil packet that held Capri Sun All Natural Strawberry Kiwi Flavored Juice Drink Blend.

- One pacifier without its nipple.
- One empty tube of Chapstick, one empty tube of lipstick, one empty tube of on-the-spot acne treatment.
- One cerise plastic razor handle with no head.
- One plastic silverware fragment.
- One plastic cigarette mouthpiece.
- One crouching plastic soldier.
- One black plastic wheel from a child's truck.
- One beat-up black pen.

It is worth noting that the character of this litter seems little different from the litter I have collected in the past, although lack of a prior scientific assessment makes me hesitate to make a definitive statement. It's true that there were only two beat-up tampon inserters this time though I seem to remember that intact ones used to be very frequent, there were many fewer plastic cigarette mouthpieces than I remember from the past, and there were no condoms. I refuse to guess what this might mean sociologically.

Focusing on the wrack, though, has allowed me for a while to evade the reality of the ruin. This year I had managed to string, along the posts that support my boardwalk, a piece of bright orange netting I had liberated once from a construction site, just after an earlier hurricane—our first after we moved here—had left our yard filled with telephone poles, four-by-eight sheets of plywood, and other floating trash much more damaging than bottle caps.

But the netting seems to have worked as I had hoped, since my neighbor's unprotected lawn now contains several eight-foot logs and some four-by-eight planks in addition to the more usual driftwood, and I have none of those. But vast swaths of the garden—I know it's inappropriate to describe a garden thirty-six feet wide as vast, but it's all relative—are covered with smaller driftwood, the kind that's good for making a fire when you're at the beach. So next time I'll string black bird-netting inside the orange construction netting and see if I can stop even more of what the river wants to leave.

Despite my luck with lumber, more was damaged in my yard than my sense of order. Nine of the twenty-two raised-bed frames—made of two-by-six-inch planks tethered to rebar driven four feet into the ground—managed to float themselves loose from at least one anchor, sawing their way up and down so insistently that they worked the rebar up out of the ground and up their tether until the rebar projected a foot or two above the planks to which it was fastened. The beds built last year were more vulnerable than those built this year—five of the former jerked themselves loose.

And then, since the water was over a foot and a half high at some point (points?) in time, it lifted the layers of salt hay with which I had mulched the garlic last fall and the newly planted onion sets this spring, and floated them throughout the yard, onto the path and the clover rondel, and onto the tops of the low hedge plants. On the riverbank there was no hay, but a heavy coating of those small driftwood pieces covered the entire lawn.

I have grieved over my garden's vulnerability to these "weather events" for years—much more than the mere destruction of a garden would seem to warrant. But it has become harder and harder to justify my grief in the teeth of global climate change, since so many people, including some who live just south of me in New Jersey, frequently have their *houses* filled with a foot or two of water. New Orleans has made self-pity even less acceptable. Since my house sits quite high, it is always untouched by floods, though, of course, if sea-level rise goes to the sometimes predicted twenty-five feet, my second floor will be waterfront. But even I am not yet prepared to worry about that.

Nevertheless, I have tried very hard to be a grown-up about the continual flooding of my land—at least partly because so many people are fed up with hearing about it. So I'm getting better at saying, "Yeah, I was really flooded, but I'll recover." But I have to admit that my most recent flood really pushed me to the limit. While the yard was filling up one Sunday, first with seven and a half inches of rain—which was a record—and then with the amazingly high tides that came with the unseasonable nor'easter, I put down the shades in my office and wrote a note to myself, "Don't look at the garden until Tuesday." That seemed a reasonable time limit since that much water would take a couple of days to soak in. By Tuesday, things would be okay.

But things weren't okay by Tuesday, or Wednesday, or Thursday. It's true that the eighteen inches of water that, at the height of the storm, filled my yard—from the boardwalk to within a few yards of my house—did begin to sink down, the only direction it can go in my bathtub yard. But alas, the continuing extraordinary tides refilled the yard for three successive days, which made each day harder than the last. And I'm afraid that despite my determination to be brave, I pinned several people to the wall and forced them to hear about my garden's drowning—again.

When the water had gone down enough that I could creep out around the edges, it was clear that there had been a lot of destruction, which as much as the slowly drying soil allowed, I began tentatively to clean up. My first day out, there were still puddles of standing water, and I made my way out to my riverbank by going through the next-door park, down onto the beach, and then climbing from there up onto my own boardwalk.

I realized I needed a broom rake to clear away the driftwood from the lawn on the riverbank (if one dare call the collection of greenery I keep cut short a lawn). So I slipped off my shoes, made my way barefoot through the yard by splashing along on the brick edge of the center path, got the rake, and carried it back out by climbing up on the wall on the north side and avoiding land altogether. Then I raked the riverbank litter into the beds there from which the river had torn some of the soil, and fit all the plastic litter I picked out of it into a bright orange plastic bag that was part of the trash. And as I neatened the chaos I began to feel, once again, the sheer pleasure of my yard. After that, I was away for a day, and when I came back the standing water was all gone, and some parts of the yard had begun to solidify.

That was the day I could really begin the recovery effort: raking the end of the path, sweeping smaller driftwood off the top of the eighteen-inch wall (confirming that the water had really been that high), and reaching out with a long broom rake from the high edges of the clover circle to rake off the river litter that covered it. And in the middle of my work that day, as I was collecting the litter I counted at the opening of this chapter, I stopped short and said, "Joan, how much time is it really going to take you to bring this back to where it needs to be?" And I realized that with the help of my wall builder Dave, who would come to reset the uplifted beds, it might end up being a total of two eight-hour days—spread over a few more to accommodate both my age and other demands. Two days!

Not a lifetime, not a season, not even a month, but two days' worth of work and the garden would be almost back to normal. All it took was my energy, which, as I have said, I don't waste at the gym. And at that moment I realized that I needed to find an optimistic phrase to answer people who asked how I had fared when my garden flooded.

Several of my friends, noticing that these watery disruptions seem to be happening to me repeatedly, have proposed a number of solutions. And—alert as I am to the likelihood that sea-level rise will make such floodings ever more frequent—I have followed up on a few of them. Like building the wall to stop the flow of water off my neighbor's land into my own in storms. I know that's working because while his land used to drain relatively quickly onto mine after his driveway filled with the water that ran up his boat ramp, the invading Hudson now sits in his yard as determinedly as it sits in mine, since it can no longer flow south into my waiting bathtub. But despite the fact that the wall works, the Hudson still comes. Dave, on his last visit to reset one end of the wall that was leaking, said with some concern, "I'm afraid it's coming right through the riverbank, Joan." And I'm afraid he's right.

What has been most often suggested is that I get a pump, a suggestion that seemed overwrought—and impractical since it would need to be located 120 feet away from the nearest electric socket. That is, it seemed impractical until this year when a pump seemed infinitely sane, however distant from an outlet. That's because this year's last big storm brought on flooding and reflooding that seemed to promise soggy soil for weeks and led me to conclude that it would be an excellent idea to pump out the water whose entry I seem unable to prevent. So I'm going to buy a pump, and hope that for the next installment of this saga, the sogginess is shortened.

One friend, whose recency among my acquaintances helps to explain his audacity, suggested, kindly I'm sure, that I needed to find another place to garden. The only reason he dares to take such liberties is because he's never been here and doesn't know my passion for this land even when soggy. My immediate impulse was to send him some pictures of the garden when it was flourishing and a terse note that said, "You don't understand. Where would I go?"

Even the morning that I picked my way down my yard—six days after the storm and finally free of standing water—and managed to find solid places to stand to rake off the clover rondel, I couldn't help wondering how I would survive if I had to leave this almost always satisfying place that seems to have found me rather than my finding it.

Where could I go that I could wake up with the sun pouring in my windows, its rays entirely uninterrupted by trees or shadows as it swings its way up the sky from its earliest appearance over the Westchester hills across the Hudson? Where else could I sit at sunset on my boardwalk and see the river and the sky ahead stained pink by the sun falling in the west behind me?

Where would I go that I could watch the rising sun tilt farther south each morning as the year wanes, until the day we celebrate the winter solstice with a giant fire in my driveway? As we consign our bad memories to the fire and bless the community garden with smoking sage, we wait for the laggard sun to show itself so we can once again reassure ourselves that we have terminated its decline.

Where would I go to stay in close touch with the moon as it waxes and wanes, its full and glowing countenance warning me not only that I might be flooded, but that I might be tempted to go outside in my nightgown and sit on the boardwalk to watch the moonbeams tracking across the river as the high water laps chillingly close.

Looking out the windows of my office as I type, I never fail to be enchanted by the long view out across the river where I see mostly woods and, at intervals, the trains that flow on tracks along the river's edge—like centipedes during the day and long fireflies at night. And much as I despise the plastic, I love the work of keeping my garden alive, even the cleaning up! So it seems to me that my hope for my life at ninety-six is something other than wishing that my land will suddenly stop flooding— because it surely won't, no matter what I do. And my wish is surely not that I move somewhere else to grow my food—though I did walk next door yesterday and ask for half a plot in the community garden, where I'll grow some potatoes for insurance this summer.

No, the way to ensure that I don't have to pick up plastic litter at ninety-six is for the United States to pass a law that outlaws the production of nonbiodegradable plastics and requires even degradable ones to be produced in colors that won't offend in the garden until they break down. A rich brown might be best.

CHAPTER TWENTY-SIX

My Obituary

I hope it doesn't sound grim to admit that I find myself reading occasional obituaries in the *Times* with the same kind of interest I can remember my mother investing in them long before she was as old as I am now. (How odd it is to realize that you have reached the age your mother was when she was old.) I think Mom was searching the obituary columns for the names of old friends in Pasadena. I, on the other hand—considering it highly unlikely that I will find a late friend among the thousands of recently deceased residents of this huge metropolitan area— usually read obituaries for their humor, their literary interest, or to find surprises like Margo Hoff's lovely portrait.

There it was: an undated picture of a handsome thirtyish woman, hair brushed back from her strong-featured face, looking straight over the camera into the future. Underneath it were the words "Modernist artist Margo Hoff died Sunday, August 17th in the Spartan, Manhattan loft which served as both her painting studio and home." And then came the next sentence, "She was 98 years old." Wow. Now that's the way to be remembered when you go as an antique, I thought—thirtyish.

In recent years I've been thinking from time to time about my own obituary. That happens when you see the lives of people much younger than you abruptly ending after decades of vigorous health. You recognize that you could depart at any time, and you ask yourself whether you want to be remembered, and if so how. Ms. Hoff's photo put me in mind of a "Happy Holidays" greeting an eighty-plus friend sent me a year or so ago, from California, where he lives with his only slightly younger first and only wife. It's a lovely photo of a young bare-chested man tenderly helping a slender blond woman in rolled-up jeans and a strapless top make her way across rocks in a stream. Written above their heads is the caption RECENT PHOTO NOT AVAILABLE.

Considering all these signs, it's now pretty clear to me that if my death notice includes a picture, it should be the one that was used on the invitation to what I called—in admiring imitation of another friend—the fiftieth anniversary of my thirtieth birthday. In it I am sitting outdoors at a restaurant in the hills surrounding Rome—with a glass of wine in one hand and a cigarette in the other—high on food, wine, and Rome, and thoughts of romance. And it should be labeled RECENT PHOTO NOT AVAILABLE.

Which takes care of the picture. But what about the text?

I've been trying to remember the saying my mom had over her bed in the Quaker Gardens Health Center in her last years. I seem to remember that it was put out by the Sunkist lemon company and said something about getting more and more tart as you aged. And I have posted on my bulletin board the comment I found somewhere: "The day I die, I want to have a black thumb from where I hit it with a hammer and scratches on my hands from pruning the roses." So I've obviously inherited my desire not to be remembered as a cute little old lady, and I hope that if someone, somewhere does write an obituary for me, it will at least be fun.

Here's how my favorite obituary to date starts: "Erudite, sesquipedalian, ebullient, chaetophorous, neo-luddite biblio-phile . . ." Not only do I love the spirited affection expressed in all that highfalutin verbiage, but, even better, there's a word in there that I'm absolutely positive I never heard before. I had to look up *chaetophorous,* and couldn't find it, but I think it means the departed wasn't bald since *chaeto* is, according to my diction-ary, "a learned borrowing from the Greek meaning 'hair,'" and *phorous* is "a learned borrowing from Greek meaning 'bearer,' 'thing or part bearing (something).'" So the dead guy was a hair-bearer.

His obituary goes on in similarly high spirits with the notification that this was a "polysyllabic-word-using, technology-doubting lover of books and knowledge," and that his survivors will be left to look up their own words. Now, that's classy. I would hope for something equally irreverent. Like the MySpace page for British novelist Ivy Compton-Burnett. She actually died in 1969 but her MySpace page says she's 102 and in a relationship. And 129 people have signed up as her friends.

CHAPTER TWENTY-SEVEN

But Did You Get
What You Wanted?

Someone who knew that I was writing about my reaction to my husband's death in this book asked me whether I had, after all, gotten what I wanted. I suppose she was asking that in regard to Alan. A hard question. To know if you got what you wanted, it's essential to know what you were looking for, and I am not, as I have learned over time, a person who imagines things ahead of time and then yearns for them. So as I reflected on this question, I concluded that I had no idea what I wanted, or expected, when I married Alan.

And then, this morning, just as I decided I had heard enough news and would get out of bed, the announcement came out of the speaker: They were going to talk about sea-level rise in the metropolitan area. I lay back down and listened. And I thought, "Now, there's a reasonable version of that question for this part of my life. Did I get what I wanted when we moved into a flood zone?"

When Alan and I first began looking for a smaller place where we could downsize for our old age, we had some vague ideas in mind—largely secondhand from something I had read about someone else's criteria. These included being within walking distance of necessities, being part of a community, near a library, and a few other things I don't now remember. And we thought for a while of Santa Cruz, California, where we had spent some time together when I was on sabbatical and Alan was a visiting professor. We had also thought of Nyack, a village south of where we lived that had both a downtown and sort of a nightlife. Both these places seemed to have some of the requisite qualities. Piermont, where we ended up, was off the charts for a while since Alan had long ago put it into purgatory—that place to which he tended to banish things that he judged to be beyond consideration, like New Jersey. His father had once gotten a speeding ticket in New Jersey, so when we were house hunting the first time, I discovered that the entire state was off limits to the Gussow family.

When we first considered Piermont, Alan explained to me that it was a Mafia town and that "no one wanted to live there." Okay. I wasn't about to dispute that, since I had never spent any time there (neither had he, of course) and I knew little about it. All I knew really was that the bus I sometimes took traveled Piermont's Main Street en route to and from New York City and the buildings there looked sort of cute. So when Alan came home one day during the time we were desultorily house hunting and said he had seen something "interesting" in Piermont, I was only marginally interested. I am rehearsing all this old news only to make the point that when I went to look at the "interesting" house in Piermont, I knew little about the village, or about the Hudson River village towns in general, and was not at all clear what it was—except for cropland—that I really wanted.

I have written elsewhere about the experience of that day, walking through a very run-down house with the nice woman who then owned it, stepping out onto a rickety second-floor deck into a chilly November wind and walking down the outside steps wondering why on earth I was there at all. The Hudson River was out front, but it was cold and rejecting, and the yard—overhung from the south by a huge willow tree—was in serious disrepair (from a hurricane, I learned not too much later—so much for warnings). And so, as I resentfully followed my chatting husband and the homeowner down the yard, I turned and looked back, and said to myself, quite inexplicably, "I have to live here."

Why? What did I want? What did I expect to get? It was only

much later that I came to realize what must have captured me: It was the long vista and the huge open sky, so familiar from my California childhood, and completely different from our suburban house fifteen miles north, so shrouded with oak trees you had to go up to Alan's third-floor studio to try to see out beyond them. So I wanted light and an open sky, and as I sit here pondering what else I wanted, I realize that at some level I probably wanted—without knowing it—the demand of physical work to save me from having to go to the gym, a remark that isn't meant to be flippant.

I spent my infancy in Southern California in the 1930s where running around outdoors was what you did all day, and I also spent my adolescence there in the 1940s, walking a long way to school and back and working, during gym class, on the skills required to meet the president's World War II physical fitness standards: a half-mile race-walk in five minutes, running bases, shooting baskets, and the like. I was equally active in college and except for seven years in Manhattan where my only exercise consisted of a lot of walking, plus plastering, sanding, painting, drilling, and sawing to increase the habitability of the cheap apartments I could afford, my work-as-part-of-life never really ceased.

Our giant Victorian house in Congers had certainly demanded work, but in the end it defeated me, since no matter how hard I worked, I could never keep up with the thirteen-room house and the half acre—and hold down a job and raise a family at the same time. But we knew when we bought the Piermont house that it would have to be gutted and rehabbed and that the garden would need to be built from scratch. And I was retiring from the university, so that all that work appealed to me. I flung myself into the gutting of the house with almost as much passion as I flung myself into creating the yard—though I confess that I sometimes left Alan inside pulling down plaster while I sat in the sun on the riverbank and cut out crabgrass.

I know that Piermont also appealed to me because it had such potential as a garden site—just big enough, visible all at once from the house—a task of manageable proportions. And whatever the yard looked like when we started, I instinctively understood what I wanted it to look like at the end—even to the pale yellow Scotch broom I foresaw waving in the wind on the riverbank. In retrospect, I suppose my subsequent Scotch broom failures could have been an early signal from Providence that I hadn't got my wants entirely right. I had the perfect place for broom, which I had grown very successfully in Congers: a rocky annex to the boardwalk in which, even before we filled the annex with rocks, I put a large plastic pot to hold a place for the broom roots. So I bought the broom and planted it. It threw out its beautiful pea-like flowers gorgeously, for one year, and then died. I tried again, with the same result, which led me, finally, to give up and try broom in the bed in front of the house, where it also died. Clearly, broom didn't like Piermont. I had to change my plans.

But with lots of hard work, hard work that for the most part I loved doing, I redistributed the plants that were on site, planted the blueberries we had brought with us from Congers, and laid out the new garden with twenty-two beds that would hold our vegetables. We were mildly flooded from time to time when there was a very heavy prolonged rainstorm, and I kept raising the parts that stayed wet longest in the belief that in the end I could keep it from flooding.

It was the early spring after the garden was really taking shape—the year after we had filled in the rocky area near the boardwalk with luscious town compost and sowed it with wildflowers and thyme, producing a result so beautiful that people came down all spring and summer to look over the fences from north and south and enjoy—it was the next year, near the Ides of March, that the first major hurricane struck.

When we woke up on the morning of March 20, the entire

yard was underwater! Before I went to bed the night before, I had noticed that the storm window that topped our cold frame seemed to be on the wrong side of the yard—I thought it had blown off and was surprised it wasn't broken. But in the morning I could see that the entire cold frame had been lifted and floated across the yard. The yard was filled with water—later I measured the high-water mark against the fence and saw that it had reached eighteen inches—in which assortments of wooden things, plywood sheets, sections of telephone poles, lumber of assorted dimensions (like four-by-fours) were floating. The boardwalk and environs were covered with smaller driftwood and other debris and the whole front of the right end of the boardwalk had been washed out; all the plants were gone. A third of the remaining boardwalk was also torn up with much of the rock fill washed out; the soil behind the boardwalk, lovingly planted with compost and wildflowers, was gone—when the tide rose at 10 AM you could look down and see the Hudson sloshing around on the inside of the boardwalk!

And then community paid off. A number of new friends came down to help, toting four-by-eight sheets of plywood and other visiting debris down to the boardwalk and giving it back to the river from whence it came. In the end we photographed two of our young helpers sitting atop an enormous pile of wood heaped on the beach at low tide awaiting the river's rise to carry it back out to sea.

Thinking back, I believe I assumed then that this was a onetime disaster, something everyone confronted at least once in life. I didn't know this was something we—and very often just *I*—would probably have to get used to. The second or third time I faced a damaging storm alone, one of our friends asked me how I could keep doing this. I'm not sure the possibility of not doing it ever sank in. Like the pain of childbirth, the memory of the last storm tends to fade as the garden reblooms. As the announcer on the radio today said about the people whose houses on the South Shore of Long Island are increasingly vulnerable to higher-than-ever tides, 98 percent of the time, it's too wonderful to give up.

So as I contemplate my yard this morning, five weeks after an all-time record rainfall and the lowest barometric pressure in years put eighteen inches of water in my yard once again, and then repeatedly flooded it for four days, as I savor its recovered beauty, and marvel once again at Nature's recuperative capacity, I have to ask myself whether I got what I wanted. I surely got an open sky and celestial things I didn't know I wanted like the sun across the river every morning. And I got a garden that would, as I had hoped, be manageable if the storms would cease and if I would give up some of my compulsions—as I have this year—to try to maintain the path in clover despite the grasses' irresistible takeover. And I certainly have my excuse for not going to the gym when I can spend from 6 AM to 6 PM working in the yard, forgetting even to eat. Did I want the heartbreak of the storms? Certainly not. I didn't know they came, literally, with the territory. Will I decide I want something else one day soon *if*—or perhaps *when*—the destruction becomes more frequent? Hard to say. I'd like the worst of what is coming to hold off until I'm gone.

One of the reviewers of my first book about creating this place, our home in Piermont, called me "an indomitable reclaimer." Even then, I guess, it was obvious. I like the phrase, and I'm surely trying to live up to it. How long do I go on? As long as I can—despite everything—manage to raise all the vegetables I need to eat on my own flood-prone property? As long as at least a couple of tomato plants survive drowning and the rats? As long as my body holds out?

Did I get what I wanted? I'm pretty sure I did.

ENDNOTES

1. Wilson, Duff. *Fateful Harvest: The True Story of a Small Town, a Global Industry, and a Toxic Secret.* New York: HarperCollins, 2001.
2. Slater, Philip. *The Wayward Gate: Science and the Supernatural.* Boston: Beacon Press, 1977.
3. Watt, Kenneth E. F. "The End of an Energy Orgy." In Joan Dye Gussow, *The Feeding Web: Issues in Nutritional Ecology.* Palo Alto, CA: Bull Publishing, 1978.
4. Ibid.
5. Gussow, Joan Dye. "Limiting Growth in a Finite World." In Gussow, *The Feeding Web.*
6. Odum, Howard T. Environment, Power, and Society. New York: Wiley Interscience, 1971, 115.
7. Ruppert, Michael C. *Crossing the Rubicon: The Decline of American Empire at the End of the Age of Oil.* British Columbia, Canada: New Society Books, 2004; Simmons, Matthew R. *Twilight in the Desert: The Coming Saudi Oil Shock and the World Economy.* Hoboken, NJ: John Wiley and Sons, 2005; Heinberg, Richard. *Powerdown: Options and Actions for a Post-Carbon World.* British Columbia, Canada: New Society Books, 2004; Deffeyes, Kenneth. *Hubbert's Peak: The Impending World Oil Shortage.* Princeton, NJ: Princeton University Press, 2003.
8. Mouawad, Jad. "With Oil Prices Off Their Peak, Are Supplies Assured?" *New York Times Outlook on the Economy,* December 3, 2005, C-10.
9. Kunstler, James Howard. *The Long Emergency: Surviving the Converging Catastrophes of the Twenty-first Century.* New York: Atlantic Monthly Press, 2005.
10. Adapted from Kunstler, James Howard. *The Long Emergency: Surviving the Converging Catastrophes of the Twenty-first Century.* New York: Atlantic Monthly Press, 2005, quoted on COMFOOD listserve.
11. Steinhart, Carol E., and John S. Steinhart. "Energy Use in the US Food System." *Science* 184 (April 19, 1974), 307–316.
12. Singer, Natasha. "Do My Knees Look Fat to You?" *New York Times,* Thursday Styles, June 15, 2006, G-1, 3.
13. Stanway, David. Tibet's tourist invasion. *Guardian Weekly,* January 18, 2008, 3.

14. Review of *The Native Tourist* in *The Ecologist* 31:8 (October 2001), 56.
15. *New York Times,* October 23, 2005.
16. http://earthquake.usgs.gov/eqcenter/eqinthenews/2005/usgnay.
17. Brown, Paul. "Melting Ice Cap Triggering Earthquakes." *The Guardian,* September 8, 2007.
18. Chapter 2. Ecosystem Services. In: Chivian, Eric. Biodiversity: Its Importance to Human Health. Boston: Harvard Medical School Center for Health and the Global Environment, 2002.
19. Barcousky, Len. *Pittsburgh Post-Gazette,* Sunday, February 25, 2007.
20. Buchmann, Stephen L., and Gary Paul Nabhan. *The Forgotten Pollinators.* Washington, DC: Island Press, 1996.
21. Ehrlich, Paul R. and Anne H. Ehrlich. *The Population Explosion.* New York: Simon and Schuster, 1990.
22. National Gardening Association. *Gardening: The Complete Guide to Growing America's Favorite Fruits & Vegetables.* Reading, MA: Addison-Wesley Publishing, 1986.
23. For a detailed accounting of exactly how what we have built would return to Nature if we were not around, see Alan Weisman's amazing book *The World Without Us* (New York: St. Martin's Press, 2007).
24. Thomas, Lewis. *Trinity Reporter* 11:1, Summer, 1980.

Joan Dye Gussow is an author, academic, food activist, and farmer, whose early experiments in year-round eating from a 1,000-square-foot suburban garden, coupled with her work as a highly acclaimed nutrition educator, helped inspire the now-burgeoning food movement.

Her prior books, including *This Organic Life: The Confessions of a Suburban Homesteader* and *The Feeding Web: Issues in Nutritional Ecology*, energized the debates about organic food, local food, simple living, and the connection between our food, our health, and our environment. Gussow is Mary Swartz Rose Professor Emerita of Nutrition and Education at Columbia University's Teacher's College, where she formerly headed the Nutrition Education Program.

She is a founding member of Just Food and The Slow Money Alliance, and has served on the Diet, Nutrition, and Cancer Panel of the National Academy of Sciences (NAS), the NAS Food and Nutrition Board, the Food and Drug Administration's Food Advisory Panel, and the National Organic Standards Board.

She lives on the Hudson River in Piermont, New York, where she continues to grow her own year-round diet.

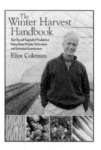